T0129899

TREASURE BAY

TREASURE BAY

FIRST BOOK
OF THE
TRADEWIND SERIES

DON A. LACKEY

TREASURE BAY
FIRST BOOK OF THE TRADEWIND SERIES

This is a work of fiction. All of the characters, names, incidents, organizations, and dialogue in this novel are either the products of the author's imagination or are used fictitiously.

iUniverse books may be ordered through booksellers or by contacting:

iUniverse
1663 Liberty Drive
Bloomington, IN 47403
www.iuniverse.com
1-800-Authors (1-800-288-4677)

ISBN: 978-1-5320-2159-6 (sc)
ISBN: 978-1-5320-2163-3 (e)

Library of Congress Control Number: 2017905768

Print information available on the last page.

iUniverse rev. date: 04/27/2017

CHAPTER 1

MOCA'S DREAM

Jon West had a huge amount on his mind, as he dozed off to sleep. His mother Moca's bed room, was close to his, and the house was now very quiet, so he could hear her snoring quietly.

In her sound sleep, Moca startled and vocalized a soft moan. A slight tremble phased through her hands, as if trying to ward off something unwanted and unsought. Her feet moved in a vague reference to running. It was the onset of a dream vision.

This, like the rare other dream visions of her life, would be a meaningful and special vision. When Moca West would awaken, it would be with that profound feeling of significance and wonderment. She would also feel confused, along with a slight tinge of something else similar to fear. This is how her dream visions always greeted her consciousness upon awakening. And her dream visions, those dreams that were non-ordinary, always manifested themselves in some fashion later on in real life!

Her longer than waist length black hair brushed across her face, looped over her shoulders then down beneath her frame. The dark of sleep opened in the middle, and spread to a panoramic view of a vast and gently rolling wheat field, waving in blending patterns as wind currents brushed over the waist high golden stalks. This was a familiar and comforting sight as she had stood atop a hill many times and enjoyed the breeze of the Kansas plains. She heard the rumble behind her, and without turning, in that dream-like way instinctively knew that a large thunderstorm loomed behind. Good, she thought, we've been desperate for rain.

Refocusing her dream reveries, she imaged back to find the wind-rippled tops of the grain stalks had become waves of water. She now looked out on an unfamiliar and foreboding sea of wind-disturbed water. The wind grew cold and became stronger as the sunlight darkened almost as night. The waves peaked and overlapped, with hissy white spew blowing from the increasing wave tops. She was frightened at this unfamiliar sea sight. She had never been off the land before, and the prospect of being in the middle of a vast and angry sea of infinite depth water engulfed her with overwhelming anguish and aloneness. In her dream she wondered, *Where did the land go ... where am I?* . She did not want to be there.

Moca turned around to see the storm again, only this time to see a deep blue gray calm sea. The storm scene part of her dream vision had ended, she dream-sensed with great relief. Still in wonderment at this water world so strange to her, she had barely time to let her dream mood transition to a calmer state, when a she looked down straight into the large round intelligent and knowing eyes of a creature she knew to be a dolphin porpoise. Her dream mood immediately calmed as a peaceful ambiance enveloped her as if transmitted into her spirit by the benevolent creature.

She realized, in a kind of dream-scene change, that she stood, or rather lay flat on her stomach, stretched out on the bow of some kind of boat, which advanced through the clear blue gray water with a galloping ease and a kind of magic power. This was a revelation: the boat moved gracefully and powerfully, but no sound except that of the water being parted as she looked down over the edge rail and saw the bow cutting ahead. She felt herself gently rise and fall as the boat moved forward with a steady purpose.

The creature had now multiplied, and become four, in the way dream things happen. In dreams, things change and you just accept them without judgement. They glided effortlessly in pairs just below the surface, a pair on each side of the bow. Each pair had one outer dolphin offset just behind and below the inner creature. As if on cue, the pairs would rapidly dip momentarily deeper and completely change sides with the other pair in a weaving formation maneuver, just missing the under-bow of the advancing hull. They were playing! She intuitively knew they were having a dolphin frolic, riding the pressure wave created under the water by the advancing boat hull, a water equivalent of the way an eagle or hawk rides the thermal wind currents in the mountains and canyons.

She studied the dolphin creatures' bodies intently. They were so strange to her. They were as large as a person, but smooth and sleek, and seemed very well suited to their environment. One had a nicked dorsal fin, a gash out of it in the middle rear. She wondered how it happened, and if it had hurt much. The creatures had a hole on top and slightly behind their heads which was normally squinched closed under water. Every so often they brushed the surface and let out a blow from the blow holes. These were strange creatures, so attuned and graceful underwater in the sea, yet needing air to breath like every other mammal. It was as if at some point in their evolutionary development, they as a species gave into their environment, trusted nature and decided to be happy wherever they were to live. Moca noted that their bottle-shaped rounded snouts cut the water well without being pointed like a swordfish. This made them look friendly and not malevolent. Their mouths seemed to be shaped slightly curved up at the ends, giving them a happy smiling look, which was not mocking in any way.

The large creature with the scarred fin seemed to roll over very slightly and gazed into Moca's eyes. Again she felt profound sense of wellbeing and peace. *They were so close!* She felt she could extend her arm and touch the creature. Moca reached out slowly ... and extended her long brown fingers, ... the creature never blinked, but maintained its steady knowing gaze in to Moca's riveted eyes, and she reached further, ... and almost touching the creatures, when ....

Moca awoke!

———◦●◦———

The week was progressing normally in the life of the West family. Oldest son Jon was busy preparing for the spring school dance at Werner High, and took endless chiding from both his older and younger sisters about his dancing abilities (or lack thereof), and also the fact that he actually had a "date". He had asked the now maturing Amy Walters to go, and she had accepted. Jon had known Amy since grade school. She was getting real fine looking, he thought, plus, she had a great personality to boot. They had been hanging out together more and more throughout this tenth grade school year. While Jon was not exactly a "jock," he did play sports, generally did well in school and was himself becoming a good looking guy.

Katie West was eleven, and was generally occupied with talking on the telephone with her girlfriends, usually gossiping about boys at school who, at their age paid scant notice to girls. Katie was highly intelligent and quick as a whip. She let nothing get past and was always one step ahead of her siblings, but always in a good-natured way. Lana, the oldest West girl, was ready to graduate this year from Werner College. Lana's beauty was striking and she had been approached more than once by most every boy in the county. However, she had never had the slightest interest in even one of them, except to allow several of the nicer ones to take her on perfunctory school dances where "dates" were appropriate. She was more interested in her studies, recreational reading and ballet.

Being duly preoccupied with graduation activities, she hadn't been around too much to join in on the usual family things. Her life was a hubbub right now, and she looked forward to the summer and the next year she planned to work at her dance studio part time. She would go to graduate school after lying out of school a year, or so was the plan.

Finally, youngest boy Kit, eight, was busy being a plain old kid. He practically worshipped older brother Jonathan, as do many younger brothers. Jonathan didn't seem to mind too much, and Kit usually stayed short of being a nuisance to Jon.

Moca was in the kitchen preparing the family dinner, and said to Jon, "What are you planning to wear to dance? Are you getting Amy a corsage? I think you should, you know."

"I'm going to wear my blue dress shirt and black slacks, Mom. And yes, I'll probably get her flowers or that mum thing." Jon knew he would have to match his peers and they were all doing that. *Seven more bucks down the drain*, he thought as he wondered about this custom; it seemed to him an unnecessary expense. "All the guys are getting their dates mums, I think." Jonathan had been industrious during his summers and saved quite a bit of money from his summer job earnings. He had spent very little of this money since his first job mowing lawns.

Jonathan had been the man of the family for a couple of

years now. His father, Sam West, had been on assignment for the government working out of the states. His exact work was classified and he had often gone away on secret assignments for unspecified lengths of time. On the last one, he had been reported missing and presumed dead. Although the family had always been loving and close, after the news about dad West, the young family closed ranks even more, and made do through the years. Moca was a Native American of Indian tribal heritage. She had a strong constitution and great inner peace and wisdom befitting her indigenous cultural heritage.

———————

Half a world away, the wind howled as a long monstrous mountain of sea passed under the sailing vessel *Tradewind*. A normal person, seeing such a thing, would be sick to the pit of their stomach and frozen with the deepest fear. The ship's brave captain, Clifton Meadows Bellwether – Capt'n "B" – watched with the experienced eye of one who knew ships and sea as well as any mariner could. *Not too bad*, he thought. *We'll weather this front and gain some way; should put us fine ahead of schedule*, he mulled. The first mate Fred, and crewman Claude Bergeron were off to the side of the bridge watching Capt'n "B".

Leaning close, Claude said above the wind, but not too loud, "He's so calm! This blow's nothing to 'em."

"Aye!" growled Fred. "He still thinks in fathoms instead of feet." Not that it presently mattered as *Tradewind* galloped over unfathomable depths of the great trackless ocean on this darkest of dark nights.

Capt'n "B" shouted, "Fred! You and Claude trim a bit o' reef in the fore jib. She keeps trying to round into the teeth of the wind. It'll ease the helm a tad and give Slim's muscles a rest." Weather helm was a bane to whoever had the helm.

Slim was helmsman on duty on this watch. He had been aboard the *Tradewind* many years, sailing the Pacific trades with Captain Pete until his passing. Captain Pete had been the Master and owner of the *Tradewind* for over thirty-five years. To bring the ship to its new owners, Fred and Slim decided to recommend Capt'n "B" to take command and deliver the ship halfway around the world.

Capt'n "B" himself moved over toward a winch and loosens a line which controlled one of the middle sails, and said to Slim, "I'm letting out the Mizzen some and that should help balance things."

The well-sealed planks creaked under the strains of the sea. Sealed and coated over with fiberglass, the *Tradewind's* hull was a wonderful blend of old and new technologies. Teak wood from Burma, Oak wood from unknown forests in the Americas, brass and bronze from English foundries, fiberglass resin and glues from some petrochemical plant which processed oil from the depths of the earth, and finally the glass itself, made of the element Silicon, same as sand and rock and it all originally came from the stuff of stars.

Fred and Claude struggled, taking in part of the sail, and setting the reefing. Hard enough in normal weather, during a blow doing anything to do with sails was dangerous, especially forward on the bow where the greatest pitching motion of the ship caused the bow to rise and fall wildly many feet as the ship ran through the waves. It was common in such conditions for crewmen to have to hold themselves down onto the deck with great strength, or be tossed into the sea by the motion.

"Better already!" shouted Fred. Capt'n "B" nodded slightly. Fred and Claude returned, but left themselves connected to the jack-line, a safety line that ran the ship's length fore and aft.

And the *Tradewind* plowed the sea on into the dark night, making miles in the wind, and onward to its new port half around the world.

CHAPTER 2

PROM NIGHT

T he big night was finally here. The music was already playing when Jon and Amy walked in the Gym. It wasn't full yet, but all their classmates were starting to show up. For some, it would be the biggest night ever, but for others it would be a non-event and in later years they would barely remember, just like most of their other high school days; one big blur. For Jon, the event was mostly going to be just a pleasant evening with Amy, one more chance to be with her and his other lifelong friends before starting their big departure from Kansas. He mostly had been down-playing it to his school mates, just saying they would be moving to Texas after school was out in June. But word had gotten out, as it always does in small towns, where everybody seems to know everything about everybody else and there were few secrets. Not that it particularly mattered, but it did irritate him.

After saying hi to a few teachers and parents who were chaperoning, Jon and Amy found a table and settled in.

Amy grabbed his arm and referring to the song being

played said, "I like this one. Come on!" pulling him half out of his barely warm seat.

———⇒●⊂———

Capt. "B" and the Tradewind round the horn of Africa.

The waves near the tip of Africa off the Cape of Good Hope were of a different character; they were huge long-space mountains of water rushing from one ocean to the other. The ship and crew handled them well, however. For Captain Bellwether, he would soon be in the Atlantic and crossing it, which would be his *first* time for that ocean, but once across, it would be that he had sailed and crossed all five of the major oceans of the world.

After rounding the Horn of the dark continent, the ocean currents dictated they stay close to the African coast up to the gold coast, then follow the currents hopping across to South America and then to the Caribbean Sea up past the Yucatan between Cuba, then straight across the Gulf of Mexico to Galveston. Easy!

Crewman Claude Bergeron and Slim were remarking to each other about current sea conditions. "We're making fine way, we are!", Claude said.

Slim retorted, "Yeah, but I'll be glad when we're away from that African coast. Not sure why, but it spooks me. I've heard about monster waves and giant holes in the water. Right around this very area too! Something about that Agulhas or Angola current."

Claude said, "I didn't want to ask Capt'n but I think we're past those currents, so just relax on that. He likes to stay out in the sea lanes about a hundred miles off shore, even when following a coast. Says it's safer and I'll go with that. I didn't want to ask him our position since that's his business. But usually ask how many days left to … uh .. the windward's, or somewhere. That tells me what I need to know. Otherwise, I don't get a Masters wage or the worries that come along with it, so who cares."

"Aye" grunted slim, who was already headed down to the galley to fix food. "Dinners in a quarter hour."

Soon enough, they hooked up with the westerly trade winds and it was a glorious hop across the sea, over to South America and the Caribbean Islands, dead across the heart of the Atlantic Ocean, following the route of Christopher Columbus and countless hurricanes, when in that season.

CHAPTER 3

UNCLE PETE'S SHIP

Captain Pete, older brother the missing Sam West, was at the helm of the *Tradewind*, making way to a port they had not often called upon; Balikpapan, Indonesia! It was Captain Pete's last voyage and he well knew it. Sensing health problems, he knew deep down it was finally time to seek health care and give up the sea-going life. And he was not all sad about it.

Balikpapan is an old port city on southeast side of the island, previously known as Borneo, in the Indonesian province of East Kalimantan. It is now politically partly called Brunei or East Malaysia. Although not on their regular trading route, Captain Pete's ship, the *Tradewind*, had called on that port numerous times over the years, and the ship had been hauled out there for repairs and maintenance several times. Now it was going for its final refit, at least as a cargo sailing vessel. Pete had learned of many maritime resources there, and he more or less thought of Balikpapan as kind of a home port in this part of the world.

It had become a fast growing city thanks to an oil boom in the region, and it had many resources, including some excellent medical centers where Pete planned on checking into as soon as *Tradewind* was refit and sent on its way to America.

Beautiful sailing weather through the South China Sea to Indonesia was most befitting for Uncle Pete's final trip. It could not have been finer.

Pete had arranged for a delivery skipper to meet them in port and take over the vessel and crew for its long trip to the United States, and the port of Balikpapan was on the horizon. The delivery skipper was a Captain Bellwether, a very experienced and trusted ships master, and himself close to retirement. He had agreed with Pete to take this voyage as a favor to Uncle Pete, plus he wanted to wind up in the States anyway, so it was a good opportunity for him.

Port was made, and sure enough, Captain "B" welcomed Pete and was right there as agreed, "Hey ye old sea spri't! How ya be Capt. Pete. Been awhile for sure." greeted the gregarious Bellwether. "The ship looks in fine shape!"

Pete replied, "She'll go over to the yard shortly for a haul out and some maintenance. Wouldn't want the new owners to have to face boat maintenance too soon." And he continued, "let's us go over to John John's Place to get a meal and talk."

Away they went, catching up, swapping tales and Pete telling Bellwether about his plans and status and other things.

John John's eatery had not changed much, except for higher prices. Pete and "B" set over in a corner where they could talk undisturbed. Pete began, "Bellwether, I'll make this short, so please just listen. I'll have yours and the crew's salaries funds, and the ship's papers and orders, in your hands from the bank tomorrow. After that, we'll not see each other again. You will stay here and coordinate with the yard on the refit. Basically I'm having them convert the cargo area back into beautiful passenger areas and enlarging the salon and galley. Also replacing all old worn fittings, block and tackle with new high quality stuff. She'll 'be a pretty sight on the seas after all that she will; and it will be your job to make the yard's men do it well and do a fine job on all that they do. I want my heirs to have a fine *Tradewind*. I covered you for about 4 months in the yard and four months in route from here to the States. So there'll be no hurry for you. Play it safe regarding the weather. The crew have a paid vacation starting now for the next month. So, thar you go ... any questions?".

Capt'n "B" replied "Naw, ya old sea buzzard, just go and get yourself taken care of. Don't worry 'bout a thing. Ya know I'll take the best care of your wishes. Have an easy mind about it. After the deliveries all made, I'm planning to stay in the States and buy a ranch out west; Probably in New Mexico. Get yourself all fixed up, and come out there and stay with me; I'll have you a bunk all set up!"

Pete said, "I know you will of course. The hours late and I'm tired, so I'll see you tomorrow.", and with that, the two parted for the night.

The next day the *Tradewind* was already hauled out and up on the ways. The project engineer had been going over Captain Pete's' refit plans and Bellwether had joined in about halfway through. When the yard's engineer had left, Pete told Bellwether, "Here, let's sit down and finish out business; Here's all the funds you'll need so keep them safe. These envelopes contain all the ships papers and transfers in the name of the new owners, and you as the new delivery master. If you don't mind, I'd like to spend a while down here alone with the old ship to tell her goodbye, in my way."

Capt'n "B" replied quietly, "I understand. You take care, and finish your worries about this part. I well have the helm now. We'll be a' seeing you old "skip"; fair winds and calm seas to you, sir!". And with that, Capt'n "B" bear-hugged Pete and left the ship, with not a dry eye.

Uncle Pete slowly and carefully paced around the main salon of the *Tradewind* for a bit, and then gently sat down on a couch, a place where he usually never sat, a place for passengers or crew. From this novel point of view, Pete, slowly looked around the cabin. He would let his eyes linger here and there, remembering many times and scenes experienced on the ship. He moved to another seat and repeated the remembering of more memories. This went on for the better part of an hour, then, he felt closure and he knew it was time for him to leave it all behind. He was not sad, but resigned and through, through and through. Pete said aloud, but softly, "Goodbye old *Tradewind*. Goodbye." Pete slowly climbed up the companionway steps to the cockpit, and at the top, he slowly closed the heavy teak wood hatch behind him and locked it up. With that, he climbed down off the ship and went to search out the health care facility where he would spend his final days. He did not look back.

———⊰•⊱———

Months passed as the ship was refit. The crew returned from their vacations. There came a day to depart and so it was.

The *Tradewind* made its way across the trackless Indian Ocean to round the Horn at the bottom of Africa, then across the Atlantic the long way through the Caribbean south of Cuba and then up thru the Gulf of Mexico to its new homeport of Galveston and Clear Lake, Texas.

———⊰•⊱———

Capt'n "B" looked up and noticed the Galveston Light was fine on the port bow. "We made it, Pete! We made it!" Capt'n "B" whispered quietly to himself. Capt'n "B" had made it across the Atlantic Ocean, for his first time and thru the Caribbean Sea and up thru the Gulf of Mexico, no small feat. He was now a Master of all oceans of the world! And this gave him tremendous pleasure. Each area of the world's oceans seemed to have their own character, in terms of wave and weather. The Atlantic crossing proved to be quiet and predictable, good things. But Capt'n "B" did not much care for the southern part up the coast of Africa. He was glad when they got past it and approached the Canary Islands and swung westward. He knew they had to avoid the calm, windless spot which lay just west of the middle of the Atlantic, sometimes referred to as the Sargasso Sea, which was a frightening bane to many old time mariners. They would be mired down in windless water desert for weeks, driving their crews to madness.

CHAPTER 4

LEAVING KANSAS

H ere were the entire West's together at the dinner table, except for father Sam West, whose chair sat there vacant and his spirit missed. He had been missing for about two years now, and had not come back from a government assignment, all unknown by the family. His duties were clandestine and they never knew the details of his assignments and travels, except that he was paid well and did work that was important to the country.

"Excited, Jon?" said Moca. "Tomorrow's the big day; we leave early."

Jon nodded, and kept eating. She knew he was about to burst from excitement. Everybody was kind of quiet, actually, but from excitement and anticipation.

Kit finally said. "Mommy, I'm kinda of scary."

"Don't be scared!" Moca said. "We'll just be driving, for a long while, just like a vacation trip. The big thing will be learning about that boat, or ship, or whatever it is."

She didn't want to even mention going out into the ocean on a boat, and all that. Like her dream had portended, that could be totally new to all of them, and really exciting and scary.

"OK, goodnight all!" Jon said getting up and heading to his bedroom. "Up early, everybody. No grumps in the morning!"

Everybody said ok or un-huh or you too. They finished gobbling their food and ambled off bed. Moca cleaned up and tried to shut all thoughts of tomorrow out of mind. Climbing into bed, thoughts of her dream vision kept coming to mind. Visions of rolling hills, distant horizons and wheat crops as far as the eye could see, and it gave her great comfort, sleep came quickly.

Kit bounded into Moca's room and slide under the covers waking her up.

"Go to sleep," she softly said to little Kit, and it was lights out.

Heather was sleeping in Lantana's room this night. Heather ask her, "Lan, how many miles is it to Galveston from here?"

Lan replied, "Well, it's going to take us 3 days to get all the way there, but we are taking our time and have a few extra stops planned."

"Oh, … ok." Heather said, closing her eyes. "It'll be fun. I always like road trips!"

As night fell, all the West's were sleeping soundly, their last night on their Kansas farm. Crickets buzzed and moonlight bathed the wheat fields and rolling hills. They didn't notice the truck that passed the farm in the middle of the night that had "Brunson Trucking" painted on the side, as it slowed passing the front gate, then went on along its way.

—————

As morning dawned, Moca's sister Netilena was first to arrive, driving up the gravel driveway and not being quiet. "Wake up everybody!" she said loudly getting out, slamming doors, and trying to be as noisy as possible. Kids poured out of the house and Nettie noticed the West car was already opened and being packed. Everybody was intent on their packing and scurrying around back and forth from house to car, checking and rechecking.

Finally everybody seemed ready and collected like a group ready to say a final goodbye, which they did, and started packing themselves into the car getting set to zoom off down the road.

CHAPTER 5

Over Land Down to Galveston

"Lan, did you get everything that you wanted into that last bag? I'll load it. I'm almost done," said the dutiful Jon to Lantana. He was a ball of energy, Jon always catering the role of a wagon train captain overseeing a crossing of the Great Plains. Not in a hounding way, but in a respectful but firm way of the natural leader he had within. Actually, he had a willing crew, since they were all excited and ready to get on the road. The family had not enjoyed a real vacation in almost forever, and this trip would be like a vacation of sorts. Moca and Jon had travelled to Washington DC on business related to Dad (Sam) and the agency, but that trip had been more focused on the circumstances of his "gone missing" and his absence. Thankfully, this trip was without that burden.

Katie, Heather, and Kit already had their nest carved out in the vehicle, with blankets and pillows and coloring books and a few important toys, and of course the music player and earphones for Katie. Even though Katie was eleven, she still had a lot of kid in her, at least when not around her peers.

Moca called out, "Alright everybody, load up!" and did yet one more sweep around the house, just making sure nothing was being left behind. Moca's sister, Netilena was going to move in and house-sit until things firmed up for the adventuring West's. They didn't want to sell the farm, for it would always be the home-place to be kept in the family. Nettie and a few neighbors had been gathering outside to send them off.

Jon tied the last of things down in the trailer, and stood just outside the car. The kids loaded up and Moca, Lantana, Jon took turns hugging and shaking hands with the well-wishers.

"Moca, you all be really careful now and call me every night, or I won't sleep," Netilena said, getting tears. They had never been far apart, so this was a very large deal.

"I will, Nettie, I absolutely will!".

"Everything here will be just fine. Don't worry about a thing and you all have the most wonderful time you possibly can. Don't forget about me, .. well all of us, but do forget about things for a while anyway, .. You know what I mean, with Sam and everything. Things will work out. And this boat thing, I just can't imagine! I'm envious in a way. Tell me everything, ok?"

"Sure Sis, I definitely will," the sisters exchanged with wet eyes but all warm smiles. And with a last long tight hug, Moca hopped in the passenger side and Jon drove them off down the familiar long straight Kansas road from the farm.

Jon was the first to speak. "You know Mom; I think we should go ahead and get on I35 instead of going down that smaller road through Tulsa. I think we'll make better time, plus there'll be more gas stops, because we'll be using more pulling this trailer and everything."

"That's fine," she replied, still lingering on Sis. She knew

Sis would keep everything in good stead, but she already she felt a hollow empty yearning twinge of that homesick feeling. I'll have to get rid of that, she directly thought, and focused on Jon's remark and started to think about the realities of the trip at hand. "Plus, if we went through Tulsa, we'd be tempted to stop to visit our cousins there, or maybe go by that Will Rogers Museum and that would waste time. Not that I've travelled that much, but I've noticed it doesn't take too many stops on a trip before you notice at the end of the day you have not covered the miles you should have."

"Mom, that's obvious," chimed Heather from the nest. She was hunkered down by Katie, both with their reading glasses on, looking professorial, already involved in a book, but also paying attention to everything.

"Mom, who was Will Rogers?" asked Kit.

"Well, I guess he was a famous guy 'back in the day', a comedian mostly; it was before my time, I've only just seen pictures."

Lan added, "I did a report on him for English. He was a favorite son of Oklahoma, and was in a lot of films and shows sometimes in about the nineteen-thirties. I think he was part Cherokee."

"Anyway, there is a great memorial museum for him in Tulsa that I've always wanted to visit," said Moca, "but now we have to make good time to Texas to meet that boat!" Shifting around in her seat, Moca began to recount, "You know, growing up I used to hear a lot of people say that everybody in Texas had an oil well. I wonder how many we'll see, oil wells that is."

Jon added, "I was looking at one of those water-maps in Uncle Pete's packet that he sent, .. I think they call them charts; anyway they showed lots of oil wells out in the middle of the water. Out in the bay, and out offshore even. I think they go down real deep. There's actually a bunch of stuff to look out for out there." Of the whole family, Jon had taken the most interest in learning and reading about nautical things, once they had received news of Uncle Pete's gift, and the coming adventure.

Lan had stopped listening and was already musing about rich oil men, and dirty, oil-smeared wildcatters and roughnecks like she'd seen in old movies. "Well, it's not like we don't have any oil wells in Kansas!" she defended.

Kit said, "If we had and oil well, we could put it in our car." Several laughed and gave him suitable affirmations. Moca reached back and loosened his seat belt to make him more comfortable. "When we get about one hour south of Oklahoma City just before Pauls Valley, I want to stop at Whitebead cemetery to visit my grandmothers' and other relatives' grave sites.

No one said word, especially the kids who didn't relate to that sort of thing anyway. Jon knew about the plan to stop there, and had already perused it on the map and had figured it into the trip plan. White Bead was an old settlement of the Choctaw Indian tribe, and the cemetery was just about one-half mile west of the I-35 freeway. What he didn't figure was that when they got there, it would be pitch dark and raining.

Moca's grandparents were both Chickasaw and Choctaw. Grandmother Sallie Patricia Spain was buried at White Bead, along with great-grandfather David McKnight Spain and his brother Beauregard, evidently called 'Burey'. Little was known about them except that they were in the great Oklahoma Territory Land Rush of April 22, 1889. It was told he (great grandfather David McKnight Spain) had won a section of land, some of which was later partly gambled away according to family lore. Still, Spain was a respected local rancher all his life and had donated part of the land for the cemetery and church. He had met and married the lovely Georgia James in those early times somewhere along the Red

River valley on one of his cattle drives between San Antonio and other regions in Texas, up through to Kansas City, or some other rail-head town. Great grandmother Georgia had been full blood Chickasaw. Moca never knew David M. Spain had any actual Indian blood until recently, but it turned out that he was most likely a descendant of Anichiihona, one of twin sisters who were in the 'royal' clan of early Choctaw leaders, nieces of the great chief actually. They weren't Indian princesses' since the tribe really didn't have such, but were the closest thing to it. David M. and Georgia had 4 girls of which Moca's grandmother Sallie Patricia was the youngest. She would attend St. Mary's college down in San Antonio, work for the post office, and love animals. Moca had picture of great grandfather David M. Spain hand feeding a wild deer on his land out on the early plains of Oklahoma around White Bead. Another sepia-toned photo was of the farmhouse, David M. and brother Beauregard and other farm hands sitting around the front porch. The look and feel of the photo made for all kinds of questions about life and times depicted. Things looked stark and it appeared the basic living was rough and tough. One of those old sepia pictures where nobody was smiling.

"Mom, am I a Indian?" Kit asked.

"An Indian, Kit honey, say 'AN Indian'," corrected Moca gently.

"Ok, AN Indian. Am I a AN Indian?"

Moca and Lantana chuckled, and Lan said, "We are all of us part Indian, but we're not exactly sure how much, like one-half, or one-fourth or even five-eighths. And that all comes from Mom. I don't think Dad had any Indian in him at all."

Jon, getting bored with the conversation, added, "I supposed that means that the most any of us kids could be, would be half-Indian at most."

Heather chuckled, "Half AN Indian!"

"Well, like Lan has Indian hair, but Jon doesn't. Or, that Mom's skin is nice and beautiful golden brown, like Indians have but Heather has whiter skin color," Jon went on.

Lantana said, "You're actually supposed to say 'American' Indian to be politically correct, or Native American, and not confuse with East Indian people from the country India."

"Yeah, but we'll just keep saying we're Indians 'cause it's shorter, and we all will know what we mean. Besides, American Indians are the only Indians we care about anyways," concluded the ever analytical Heather. "She began to jab and tickle Kit and added, ".. and I'm going to wrap a turban cap on your head so people will think you're that OTHER type of Indian." Making her hand karate-chop flat, she saw-motioned Kits little tummy saying, "Maybe I'll even saw you in two, making you half AN Indian!" And then two became a ball of laughing giggling siblings in their car-nest, while Katie quarter-turned her back on the silliness, but threw a hard over-the-shoulder glance at the wiggling giggling two, feigning disapproval, then turned back to her book.

Moca quietly reveled in all this, knowing that such family moments were bonding and priceless; she only longed for Sam to be present to complete the picture. She could not let her mind go there, though, right now. There was too much other responsibility to shoulder right now, rather than indulge herself through obsessing about what in the world had happened to him.

They had been on the road now about four hours and it was time for a rest break and food. They were going along nicely, and were well out of their normal travel territory. The land began a subtle change towards the unfamiliar. Taking scope of business establishments in the next small town, Moca suggested, "let's stop over at that eating place; it looks quick."

Jon wheeled in, being careful of the trailer. He had been used to driving with a trailer for many years now on the farm. Country kids regularly drive on the land and county roads during farming season to help out, and drive tractors, trucks, pulling equipment and trailer, all long before they get actual official drivers licenses from the State.

They all got out stretching legs and visiting restrooms, while Moca ordered hamburgers and fries. It was an outdoorsy type place, not crowded, with picnic tables for customers and an order and pick-up. It was like a million other old mom and pop road places, the precursors to the Dairy Queens and McDonald's, except the food was usually much better than those chains. Other customers were coming and going, locals, farmers, truckers and other random folk. These were the type places, along with smaller service stations, and strip motels, that tended to populate the secondary highways and byways of middle-America. They reminded Moca of the true and more real America, the country of the dust-bowl, the "Mother" road known as U.S. Route 66, and Americana and the nineteen twenties through the fifties that she had learned about and only partly experienced through her growing up years and the conversations of her grandparents and parents about those times. This was going to be a good experience for the kids, she thought.

She paid for the order, and turned to walk over to the picnic tables to wait.

"Hi miss. Been followin' yo'all fo a little while. Noticed all tha' stuff in yo trailer. Movin'?" said a man who had just walked up behind her at the window. He had tattoos on his arms under a white t-shirt and trucker pants and trucker boots. She'd not noticed anyone following out on the road, but then there were lots of trucks. He seemed friendly, she thought, but then she felt hesitant for some reason, not sure why, to tell much detail. She glanced toward the road and saw a

large eighteen-wheeler rig parked, diesel still running. It said "Brunson Trucking" on its sign.

"Visiting relatives," she nodded to the burly man. He was between the window and the table she was going. She kept walking, making a wide path around the man, hoping that would be that, and sat down just as Jon and Heather appeared.

As they were sitting, she saw the man approach and he said, *"Gonna get me a quick burger too, then back to it. A man's gotta break eva once't in awhile. Which way you all headin'?"*

The rest of the kids were now at the table, and little Kit innocently chimed back "we're going to Galveston to get a boat and live on it!"

Katie jolted Kit with her knee out of sight below the table. She had immediately sensed her mother's discomfort with the stranger and was going to quiet Kit by her sisterly means. Jon noticed all this, but held back to see what developed next.

"How 'bout that, I'm goin' to Galveston too," grinned the man. *"Names Roy, but they call me Bear. Yup, I'm out of Chicago with a load to down there; do it all the time. Back and forth. Maybe I'll be with you all on the road for awhile."* He looked directly at Moca and added, *"Little lady, yo sho' do have a nice lookin' set of kids here. Real nice! And you too, ma'am!"*

With that, Jon got up between the man and his mother and said, "Mom, our orders ready. Why don't you go get it and I'll stay here," which she did. He said to the man, "Probably not, we have some stops to make and just enjoying our trip. So have a nice trip."

"Ok, son, you all be real careful now. Nice talkin' to you folks," and turned to leave with his bag of food, and ambled toward the big running truck.

Moca returned with the food and distributed it out to all her birdlets, who were grabbing and stuffing the good old road food. Moca quietly said to Jon, "That guy! Gave me a funny feeling. He just seemed too nosey, I think. But maybe just lonesome being friendly. I think he creeped-out Lana too."

"I don't know Mom, I didn't like the way he look at you and Lan, or something." Jon protectively replied. They finished eating their burgers, and Jon said, "Last bathroom call, then let's go."

Back on the road, they were heading into the afternoon. It looked like they would clear OK City well after rush hour traffic. Moca had the map out trying to figure the best way to navigate the freeways in the big town, even though they had a ways to go. On the way, they crossed the state line, the first time for most of them.

"Oklahoma!" exclaimed Heather spotting the huge sign at the Visitor Center.

Kit mimicked cutely, "Yeah, Oakahoma!"

They had to get out and pose for a family picture in front of the sign, like tourists do. They did not even notice the big "Brunson Trucking" rig roll past on the freeway. They weren't in Kansas anymore!

They rolled on toward Oklahoma City uneventfully. The smaller kids had been napping, and Moca had taken over driving for awhile. Jon even zoned out for a spell, but awoke as they approached the big town. They changed drivers again, so that Moca could navigate while Jon drove. It was getting dark. It also looked like rain ahead on the other side of the City. Once past downtown and out on the south side, they stopped for a break. After a short stop, they were back going, and they drove into the storm. It was mild by comparison; not a violent front line type storm that bred tornadoes, but enough to generate pelting rain and lightning. Moca was driving, slowed to 50 and put on flasher lights. Trucks passed and spewed torrents of water blinding the windshield for what seemed like too long for Moca. It begin to let up a little, just as they approached Pauls Valley. "Ok here's the White Bead exit," Jon said to his mother, as he studied his road map. "Just go up and turn right and go about one half mile or so then right again on Kimberlin road, according to the map."

"I kind of remember," said Moca. "There's a horse rescue farm just across the road." It was pitch dark, no moon, no stars, and lightning not far away as the storm still rumbled, and rain on and off. The cemetery gate was spotted and they carefully pulled in. "Go to the right, and go around and the graves are in the middle somewhere. I'll recognize them."

Lana remarked, "How spooky a night to be in a cemetery!" Nobody protested too much, however, since they knew this was important to Mom. Respect was given freely in the West family and boundaries were respected as well, a golden trait in today's world, an observer would think.

Moca got the big high-beam light out and began scanning the grave sites as Jon drove slowly down the middle isle. "There! Go ahead and stop, but leave everything running. I'll get out and go look. One thing she needed were names and dates from the headstones for some family genealogy work she loved to do. And also, she was convinced there must be some missing names from her family tree that surrounding markers may give clues and missing links. Genealogists love cemeteries, thought Moca, as she climbed out into the night.

Everybody in the car caught a nap while Mom was out scouting headstones. After about twenty minutes, Moca felt completed, having taken pictures and done the paper-scratching thing on a number of the headstones. Plus a piece of the storm was moving back in, lightening coming closer and rain starting. Everything seemed in order. She heard a noise out toward the back of the cemetery, and looked up just in time to catch a man's silhouette back-lit by a lightning strike. There was a MAN out there! She turned off her beam, and ran back to the running car, hopped in the driver's side and went as fast as safely possible out of Whitebead Cemetery.

On the way out, on the far side of the cemetery opposite from where they came in, there was a large rig parked IN THE CEMETERY. They had not noticed, or couldn't see it coming in because of trees, the dark and the storm. But the writing on the truck said "Brunson Trucking"!

Both Lantana and Jon had awakened by now, and all three saw it. But nobody said anything. In few minutes, Lan said, "Just keep driving fast, Mom, just keep driving and don't stop for a long time!" Jon was looking backward to keep watch. A ways down the freeway, way back in the dark night he thought he saw vehicle lights entering the freeway from the same entrance, the only entrance for miles.

In a low anxious tone, Jon added, "Yeah, Mom, just keep driving!"

CHAPTER 6

CLEAR LAKE

They had taken the freeway right through the heart of downtown Houston, giant skyscrapers, glass buildings and zooming traffic on unending freeways. The map showed only a few more miles to go south of the city, where the Clear Lake marina district lay about halfway to Galveston, but about one hour away due to traffic.

To say that the Clear Lake area is a colorful place to live was an understatement. There was so much going on that the whole scene was kind of hard to get a hold of. Clear Lake was a large residential area nestled on the western edge of Upper Galveston Bay and there actually was a Clear Lake which was neither clear, nor very deep, nor very big. It was actually an estuary lake at the end of Clear Creek and some other small tributaries just before it all dumped into the bay. In fact, once during the winter of 1982, a persistent norther blew ALL the water out of the lake and one could walk across it. There was a small dredged out channel for deeper draft sailboats to use which ran the length of the body of water. Clear Lake and its surrounding community town-lets were home to NASA, lots of aerospace contractor companies, some petrochemical plants and the fourth largest concentration of pleasure boats in the United States. In sleepier days, the area was sparsely populated with much vacant land, forests, shack-let camp type huts that were weekend getaways, and fishing boats. The lake was now surrounded by high-end marinas, condominiums, hotels, businesses and expensive homes behind gates.

One of the first big hotel-marina complexes there was the Safe Harbor hotel and marina. It was safe and fancy, and that is where the incoming *Tradewind* would call home port. It had great accommodations, being right in the middle of all the new activity and business development which was transforming the formerly sleepy little community into a thriving and growing recreational area and major suburb of Houston. Safe Harbor Marina had nice wide floating docks which rose and fell with the tide, so the boat was always the same height from the dock, definitely a good thing. The place also had a great fantastic swimming pool. It had a swim up bar and two islands in the luxurious pool complete with palm trees.

The Wests converged on the Marina's business office. The secretary said, "Hi folks, what can I do for you?"

Jon and Moca went into the manager's office and sat down while the rest of the kids stayed with the secretary in the outer office.

"We want to rent a place for a boat." Moca said, and proceeded to explain the particulars. The secretary said, "OK, You want a SLIP. Come this way into Mr. Szafir's office. Fred Szafir is our Harbor Master and he handles all our leasing. Just have a seat and wait." The secretary places some paperwork down in front of them and provided a pen on top of that adding, "If you all will just get started on this information, I'm sure he'll be along shortly. He just went out to look at something on the docks with another tenant."

Sure enough, before long Mr. Fred the harbor master came in the front door and they heard the secretary say "Mr. Fred, there are some new tenants in your office."

Mr. Fred popped into his office and introduced himself. "So! Are you all Texans or where are you from?"

Moca gave him a quick run-down and a description of the boat and their dock needs, as best she knew them at this time.

With that, Mr. Fred was up and looking at his wall layout of the marina and he said, "I think I'll put you on Pier 3, Slip 33. That's about half way down the pier, let's walk down there and you'll see it."

After that they finished the paperwork and went to eat. They found a place called the Shrimp Hut, where you ate outside under large umbrellas on large picnic tables. Very informal and fun.

Moca said, "Wow, this food is great! There is nothing like Gulf fried shrimp." as she delicately picked another delicious battered shrimp in her fingers and put it to her lips. "Just right!" biting it half in two.

"And crinkle cut fries too, my favorite!" Said Kit.

CHAPTER 7

LANDING IN GALVESTON

"**S**lim! Galveston sea buoy off the port bow," shouted
Claude Bergeron, who was up on the bowsprit
with the powerful wide-field military specification
binoculars. Clear of traffic otherwise. Just bring'r in as she
goes and take her down the middle."

"Aye, mate. Come on back and start making ready the
dock lines and fenders." Slim called back. It was way too
early to do the dock lines but they had been at sea for months
and were good and ready to make port. The Gulf, being
bowl shaped, was a choppy sea to sail, unlike the more
long comfortable wave of the major oceans and the South
Pacific Sea.

Fred was coming up from off-watch and it was all hands
on deck for the final approach. The great Galveston Light lay
ahead just on the horizon slightly to port of their course true.
All the crew had become anxious and ready.

Unlike most other coastal parts of the world, there were
many offshore oil rigs along the Texas and Louisiana Gulf
Coast and a lot of tanker traffic. Houston, just up the Houston
Ship Channel past Galveston, was a major seaport. It used to

be Galveston in the 1800s, but the 1901 hurricane that wiped out Galveston changed all that.

Capt'n "B" approached the helm and said, "Slim, I think we're fine on deck for at least forty-five minutes. I'll shout when I need a watch as we make the Jetties. Take the crew and go below and start cleaning up everything nook and cranny. Stow all of your gear good and away. When we first dock, they're going to pour aboard like roaches and I want them to see a ship shape vessel now."

Although not obsessive like a Captain Queeg of the fictional Caine Mutiny, Captain Bellwether did not like an untidy ship and the crew knew it. They did a pretty good running job of keeping orderly and neat, so there would not be that much to do except routine cleaning and stowing away.

Slim gave the helm to "B" and went to round up the crew. They all smartly disappeared below to start the assignment. Slim issued, "Fred! Claude, be sure to round up your girlie magazines!" As they all laughed and got busy; they knew the drill well. They were a fine crew indeed, and got along through the thick and thin of voyaging at sea. Even a large ship could quickly become very small when people didn't get along and pull their weight fairly.

Capt'n "B" was alone on deck now. Gazing ahead, he could see a couple of tall buildings on the island. From studying the charts, he knew the Jetties were canted more east-to-west rather that north-south, so they had a little zigzag to do, but the southeast wind was fair to all approach courses today, so no problem. He had not sailed to a busy U.S. port in many a year and was anxious a little. Bolivar Roads as it was called, was one of the busiest maritime crossing points in the world, with no less than five major heavy commercial marine waterways intersecting within a one mile area. The heavy marine vessels crossing there consisted of push or tug boats towing many oil barges, major large container ships, large oil tankers, Coast Guard vessels, and oil service boats. It was especially scary at night, and you better recognize marine light patterns well and have your wits about you.. But it was daytime and his vast experience and excellent seamanship would stand well and it went fine.

———⟫●⟪———

On shore, all the Wests were just finishing with lunch at one of the famous seafood restaurants on the Galveston seawall. The sea wall was a man-made concrete and granite structure 12 or 15 feet high to protect the island from the onslaught of the sea during storms, such as the hurricane that destroyed the island in 1901. A large roadway ran atop the seawall, appropriately named Seawall Boulevard, which was the original tourist area of the island; a natural draw of sea and sand, boardwalks, fishing piers and tourist shops. The Wests had dined at the Seawall Restaurant, one of the many facing the Gulf, and were walking out to enjoy the day.

The ever-observing Heather was the first to spot the sails on the southern horizon. "Look! Look everybody; I think that's our ship, those sails way out there! See? I bet that's *Tradewind!*" she exclaimed as she pointed, spun and danced.

They all stopped and studied the horizon.

"Maybe. Probably," Jon said. "Let's hurry on to the Harbor Master's office and see if they are on the radio yet. I'll bet it's our boat!"

———⟫●⟪———

Floy Kinell was the office-running secretary to the Galveston Harbor Master, Howard Brady. Howard was a capable man young enough to be Floy's son and had been in the office about two years. He was previously a Galveston

Channel Pilot and had ferried many a large vessel and floating oil rigs in and out of the occasionally crowded harbor. But Floy had been secretary for over twenty years and knew the smallest detail of the operation inside and out. The job was her life especially since her husband passed away five years ago.

As Floy sat at her desk doing a daily report, the door flew open as a crowd of West's clamored in.

Moca offered breathlessly, "We're the West family and we have a sailing vessel coming in and we think it's out over the horizon, the Jetties, out there! Can you call it on the radio? Do you have a way?"

Floy complied, "Sure just a second." Quickly finishing the report, Floy threw it in the out basket and said, "OK, now what is the vessel's name?"

"*Tradewind,*" said Heath.

"And just what kind of vessel is it now? A fishing boat ... pleasure boat or what?" asked Floy getting amused.

"It's our sailboat from Uncle Pete'" blurbed Kit.

Jon said in a more commanding tone, "Ma'am, it's the sailing vessel '*Tradewind*' arriving here from the South Pacific. There's a professional crew aboard. Captain Bellwether is in command. We're the new owners, and we're taking delivery and will be staying here for a few days, then sailing on up to Clear Lake to permanently berth at Safe Shore Marina. Oh, and my name is Jonathan West."

Heather glanced at Katie with raised eyebrows since Jon never referred to himself as 'Jonathan'.

"OK then, Jonathan," Floy said, turning to a counter behind her desk, "let's try hailing them on channel 16 on the VHF."

"Channel one six Galveston Harbor Master calling the sailing vessel *Tradewind*, the sailing vessel *Tradewind*; come in channel one six, over," Floy called into the desk mic." A few seconds past and she repeated the call exactly.

Jon was studying all the equipment, and especially the detailed nautical charts of the harbor and the jetties area, while Heather and Katie were still whispering and giggling about Jon referring to himself in such a stilted manner. Moca put her hand on Jon's shoulder and waited expectantly for the crackling speaker to respond.

"Galveston Harbor, this is the sailing vessel *Tradewind*; repeat this is *Tradewind*; Capt'n "B" here; go ahead. Over."

"*Tradewind*, we have people in the office here waiting for your arrival. You can dock up here in front of the Harbor Master office under the sign, or go straight to the T-head end of Pier 2 just past the office. What is your preference? Over." asked Floy.

"Galveston Harbor, *Tradewind* -- can we pick up some diesel in front of the office? If so, we'll come into the fuel dock by the office. Over." Replied Bellwether.

"Affirmative. That is affirmative *Tradewind*. We'll see you shortly. Galveston Harbor Master; Over and out." answered Floy.

"*Tradewind* clear, channel one-six, out" ended Bellwether on the VHF.

Floy could tell about how far out they were just by the signal strength and clarity on the radio. "Your boat is just about 15 minutes away, guys," she said to the group. "Y'all can wait around here. Restrooms and coke machine's around back and there's some benches and cool shade out to the side. Let me know if you need anything else."

Moca directed the group, "Let's go outside and wait crew. Thanks Miss! Appreciate your help. I'm sure we'll be seeing more of you around."

"No problem." Floy said smiling. "Can't wait to hear about their crossing and other tales."

"Us too!" Said Moca, while herding the tribe out the door. Outside, Jon looked around while the others except Moca scattered, and said excitedly, "I guess they'll dock right here to take fuel. We can board and go over with them to the other pier right over there when they are finished. It'll be our first ride!"

Galveston Channel was a very busy place indeed; Shrimp boats, oyster boats, loud noisey oil service boats of all shapes and sizes, giant oil tankers passing by, all manner of pleasure yachts and private fishing boats, Tug or "push" boats with barges full and empty. It was a real melee. There was a vessel at the fuel dock just finishing fueling, and Jon said to the crewmen, "Where you all going?"

The man replied, "Out to the Flower Gardens; a diving trip. It's a place about two hundred miles south of here where the bottom comes up to about 60 feet and there's a coral reef; it's a beautiful dive spot, if you're into that sort of thing. One of the northernmost reefs in this part of the world, or something like that."

A lot to know, thought Jon. He did not remember seeing a "Flower Gardens" marked on the nautical charts, but he would now look closer.

"You can't drop anchor out there ... too deep and it'll damage the reef, but there are some permanent mooring buoys out there to tie up to." The man said.

"Thanks for that info!" said Jon. "Sounds like an interesting spot." He already had several interesting sounding places in mind to visit and this would be one more.

CHAPTER 8

WELCOME ABOARD

C aptain "B" and all the crew finished tying the dock line and other chores, then lined up. Bellwether look at the Wests and authoritatively said, "I be Captain Bellwether. Are you the West Family?"

"Yes Sir", replied Moca. The rest were too scared to speak.

"Well, welcome aboard then come on up" Bellwether said dropping some of the pretense and donning a warm smile. The crew broke rank and started helping the smaller ones over the rail and lifelines.

"Wow" Jon said under his breath, "Look at this! She's magnificent!"

It was almost too much to take in. Moca noticed the color and textures of the woods, how decks were battened teak wood, cleaned and bleached and a small bead of tar pitch sealant between each of the one-inch wide boards. It felt solid and good under her bare feet. She had left her leather-soled shoes on the pier. The handholds were finely finished varnished teak, with a deep shiny coating. Then there were a few painted areas, like inside the cabin, the roof, and cabinets. Immediately Moca and the girls went down below.

Quickly they surveyed the galley, the main salon common living area, and then the cabins and bunks. Moca right then and there assigned the cabins and sleeping bunks for each person. Then each one started opening and closing the myriad of cabinets, hatches and shelves, just to see how big they were, what was in them and to figure what they could store there.

Jon stayed topsides and slowly walked the deck exploring. His eyes took in each item that made up a working sailing vessel, every one having a specific function in the scheme of things. A winch for this, a line for that, and pulley's, called blocks in ship-talk, the same with ropes which were called "lines", shackles and fittings and much more. There were no ropes on a boat, only "lines". The gear was all a little overwhelming but highly interesting to Jon. Claude Bergeron walked behind him naming a few things as they went. Captain "B" had disembarked and walked into the Harbor Master's office to take care of official business and make fueling arrangements.

Floy looked up to see the neatly trimmed bearded man walk in. He thundered, "Ma'am, I'm Captain Bellwether of the sailing vessel *Tradewind* just docked. We'll be taking fuel before we move over to our pier if that's ok. I'll be paying cash, but will need a receipt." Bellwether noticed that the person behind the desk was a well-preserved lady about his age. Her long hair was swept into a ponytail and was a rich gray with some flavors of brown mixed. She had a youthful aspect to her appearance, despite her age.

He was glad when she stood and broke into a charming smile and said, "Captain Bellwether, we spoke on the radio. Good to see you! And I want to hear about your trip. You delivery skippers always have such interesting stories to relate." Floy immediately notice how tall this man was. She instinctively glanced at his hands and noticed they a perfect specimen. She had a thing about hands; didn't like short stubby ones or those overly big clumsy looking thick hands, or skinny pointy hands. No, they had to be just right, and his were. Floy walked past Bellwether to get some paperwork for the Captain to fill out.

"Captain, if you and your crew would like to shower, there's good facilities right behind this building in the bathhouse." Floy said, and added, "I'll get the boys started on the fuel."

Bellwether finished the paperwork and went back outside. "Mates, there's showers back there. I'm going to clean up, and you all can too. Before we take her out there to the end of Pier 2 over there." he said pointing. With that he went below to get his bag and then back up and off the ship.

The West's had all gathered back on deck and continued to inspect their new floating home. By this time, Jon had moved behind the giant helm wheel that had steered the ship across oceans. He carefully placed his hands in the ten and two o'clock positions and stood with his feet apart. With small force he tried to turn the huge wheel.

"She's helm locked boy!" Slim said as he jumped off the boat to head for the showers. "Unscrew that lock midway down the binnacle to unlock her."

Jon looked down and loosened the helm-lock and the wheel was free in his hands. *"Binnacle"* He said aloud., and silently thought *I read about those. "Meant to cover and hide a compass in the old days from ignorant non-sailors on the dock who might stroll by and think it was witchcraft and burn up ship."* After playing with it for a moment, he re-centered the helm and locked it back. That was his first lesson.

Heather was watching all this, and said, "How did it feel Jon".

"Good. Real good." Answered Jon. "Here, come try."

Excitedly, Heather took Jon's place and went through the same drill.

CHAPTER 9

THE FIRST NIGHT ABOARD

This day was as exciting as any Jon could remember. He wonder what lay ahead.

"Look at that! The magic hour they say," exclaimed Moca. "And Jon, if you'll go down and start chopping the two onions, I'll start peeling the shrimp. Kit can start the fire and we'll try that barbecue grill thing hanging out over the, uh?"

"The rail mom, they call it the rail. Actually, the lifelines on the rail or the stanchions; You could also say "over the stern." Jon said sheepishly, beginning to see the humor in his new but untested knowledge. He knew he was still learning and had not quite gotten all the terms exactly straight, or how experienced sailors used them. "But sure, I'll go down and do that right now! I could eat a horse."

Moca came down to the galley and wrapped some potatoes in foil, peeled shrimp and wrapped them in bacon with a toothpick stabbed through. Perfect for barbecuing. Jon opened a bottle of wine for Moca and drinks for the kids. All went on deck and when the fire had done its job, all were served on deck just as the sun sank below the horizon.

"Here's to you mom!" Jon toasted as all the West family

tinkled their glasses together in a toast. "Our first night aboard. There'll never another first night!"

"Yeah mom! Our first night board!" chimed Kit, who had a shrimp in his mouth, one in his hand and barbecue sauce smeared all over his face.

Katie was already on it. Wetting a napkin, she reach over cleaning Kit's face, she said "Kit, it goes in the mouth not the face!" laughing at him. Kit was compliant with Katie's mothering him. They had always been that way since Kit was born. Heather would look on and observe and comment, but Katie would take action, but it was all natural and ok.

The meal was a fine first meal aboard ships. Fire-baked potatoes with onions and butter, peas, and the bacon-wrapped barbeque shrimp with BBQ sauce were out of this world.

"I think food taste better on a boat." Observed Lantana. "It's easy and simple but good. When I get to college, I'm going to do this same meal for my dorm-mates. I'll be the hit of the dorm!"

Moca said "Well, just make sure you use fresh gulf shrimp. Tens! That means heads on, ten shrimp to the pound. And make sure they have that reddish color and smell fresh."

"Mom, do you think there are any spiders or bugs in our bunks?" asked the ever thinking Heath.

"Or maybe a crab will crawl up and come inside and pinch you!" laughed Kit.

"No!" replied Moca, "We've cleaned and sprayed out everything super-clean. There's not a bug to be found, and crabs can't climb, so sleep tight and don't worry. And each bunk has a light you can flip on to read or whatever. But don't go to sleep with them on. They'll run down the ship's battery."

"Actually mom, we have shore-side power and the charger–converter power supply is always on, so we can't run down the battery as long as we're plugged into the dock power," continued Jon, "and the 12volt DC circuit runs parallel to the 110 volt ac and.."

"JON! Cool it!" Katie firmed.

"Jon, What's a volt", ask Kit.

"Kids, off to bed. Now!" Moca spoke firmly.

The kids were excited but tired after a full day. They'd climbed on and off the boat a million times, explored every nook and cranny, climbed liked monkeys, ran up and down the dock, explored the marina, and met everyone that would talk to them. They even fished a little off the dock.

"Ok mom, I'll take this stuff down and wash what needs to be washed. Come kiddo's let's go below and go to bed." Said Lana, as all clamored down the companionway, off to a new adventure of sleeping on a ship. They had already decided who had which bunk, and that would be 'their' bunk. In fact they had already personalized them that day soon after they came aboard. Each bunk had little storage spaces good for storing away lots of personal items, books, alarm clocks, and things. Heather and Katie shared the forward cabin, which had overlapping v-berths. Kit occupied a pilot berth in the main cabin because he was the smallest and couldn't fall out of it. Jon had a starboard side berth near the instruments and chart table and Moca had the port side rear cabin, which had a nice luxurious rear bunk and private head.

Since Lana was going off to college soon, she slept on a couch in the main salon. There were plenty of sleeping spots in the main salon cabin for occasional guests and friends. There were also some other crew berths way up forward, and in one crew cabin, if were needed. The main salon had been greatly enlarged and much of it used to be a cargo hold for Uncle Pete's Pacific South Seas island trade business. Before he died, knowing he would be sending the boat on for other uses, he had a fine conversion job done by his favorite boat yard in Indonesia, one of his favorite ports of call.

———✥———

Jon was watching the twilight sky, a scant few clouds silhouetting, darkening blue to the east and that pinkish blue to the west. "Ah, finally quite." said Jon, and noted and old sailors adage he had recently learned in his reading about maritime things, "red sky at night, sailors' delight, red sky in morning, sailors take warning."

Moca sipped her almost empty wine glass. Her mind had been drifting to thoughts of Sam, her missing partner, mulling what he would be thinking about all this and where he would be sitting, how he would be touching her affectionately and occasionally, increasingly, as things settled into the relaxed part of the day. Her major grief had finally subsided, but oh how she missed him. Clearly, that part of her heart was torn away. "Jon? What do you think now that we've seen this thing and spent a day on board? And what do you think Dad would think?"

Moca always included Sam in their daily conversation with the kids. She kept him alive in their minds and hearts. It was a good way of coping with the terrible situation of his mysterious missing. Sam had been away on many missions before. Moca and the family never were privy to mission details. This one must have been really special though, knowing how he acted between the lines before he left. Intuitively, she had the distinct impression that this mission was very different somehow, but not an especially a dangerous one. She never doubted Sam would return as usual, but then that was two years ago.

"It'll be fine mom. I've read and studied a lot about it, and I'll keep reading. Now, there'll be lots of people to ask about things and go sailing with and get actual experience. Plus, Captain "B", Fred, Claude and crew will be here for a while and they'll teach us a lot. Old Uncle Pete saw to that just fine!" "I know, you'll be a great skipper for us, I know. I know because you have so much of your Dad in you. He was so good at everything he did." Moca said quietly as she looked away into the night and resumed her thoughts about Sam.

Jon felt the mood change. He knew the look and moved away to the rail to give his mother space for her private thoughts. He had a deep sense that this was an essential gift of respect he could grant his mother; her quiet space to keep Dad alive in her thoughts. Jon stood at the lifelines and gazed out seaward. The wavelets twinkled and the stars were now up. A magnificent star-filled night had unfolded. "Mom, this is so different that Kansas, It's so peaceful and somehow right, here, all things seem connected." He turned to find himself alone on the deck. Moca had quietly disappeared below. He stood there a long time thinking and just letting his mind freewheel. There was too much ahead to even grasp, so Jon finally let go and just took in the totality of it all. He sure was not in Kansas any more!

———⟫◆⟪———

Later, Jon was below getting used to his bunk space and settling down for some rest. It was awesome. The berth was intended for the ship's captain in that it was well positioned to quickly get up the companionway to the deck, or you could sleep there, open one eye, and view all the ships dimly lit electronic instruments for speed, position, and other navigational, radar, radios, and information necessary to perceive in an instant a sense of the status of the ship underway, while someone else was topsides on watch at the helm. It was cozy and in a position in the ship that had the least sea motion. It was not the biggest bunk, a cozy double, but it was the right bunk for him. Sleep arrived quickly as he snuggled down.

———⇒►●◄⇐———

"Jon, I'm scared, the boat's moving!" Jon heard Kit say waking up and hurrying to Jon's bunk. The boat was gently rocking and bumping against the dock. Jon look at the clock and it was 2:20am, or 0220 military time. A clap of thunder exploded nearby heralding a mild thunderstorm.

Jon told Kit, "It's ok; it's just a small thunderstorm that'll pass shortly. Here, I'll take you back and tuck you back in your pilot berth." With that, Kit was ok.

Katie had awakened and appeared in time to escort Kit back to bed. "Come on tike, let's go. I'll tuck you in. No need to be afraid of the old storm, It's just rain to make the wheat flowers grow remember?" said Katie.

Jon put on a slicker and went topsides. He saw no surprises. Slim was up too, checking the dock lines and bumpers that rested between the boat's hull and the dock.

"Sometimes they work their way up in a blow, but ev'thing's ok now. Goin' back below. See you in the morn." Said Slim.

"OK!" replied Jon and also went back down. As Jon lay there, it seemed like the whole boat was a giant cradle gently rocking everybody aboard in their bunks. "Our first storm on the boat. Not bad." He thought. As he approached sleep, the face of the girl Talia popped into his thoughts. Her eyes spoke to him some way, but he was yet sure how. He loved the way she moved, her hand gestures, the set of her fingers, the way she stood. What was it about that girl. "Oh well," he thought, "I'll just have to be around her some more until I figure this out." As that picture flew away, thoughts of sailing returned and with that, he was out.

Heather and Katie were nestled in the forward cabin. "Heath, do you think we'll fly out of these bunks in a storm?" asked Katie. The bunks overlapped kind of like bunk beds, and had a small vertical lip of wood that you had boost over crawl in. But it seemed doubtful that the lip would keep someone in during rocking and rolling of the ship. At this time, none of them had any concept of just how wildly rough it could be in a real violent storm at sea.

Katie had the top bunk.

"Hey look. Feel underneath your mattress. That heavy canvas thing you feel is a lee cloth. During rough weather, you take it out, and attach the top hooks to the ceiling hooks and it keeps you in." taught Heath.

"How did you know that?" said Katie.

"Oh, I read it in one of Jon's sea books the other day." Heather said in a matter of fact tone. "Read some other stuff too. I'll tell you as things come up. You know the guys don't know everything!" They both looked at each other and laughed, as sisters who have spent a lifetime of bonding do.

"I do really wish Dad were here." Heather said. "But Jon is going to take care of us just fine, I'm sure. But I'm going to know what he knows and be his second, I think. Best I can anyway."

Turning off the lights, Katie answered, "I know you'll both take care of us. And mom will too. I think Dad will come back someday, do you?"

"Well I hope so, but I don't know. Seems like if he were alive, or could come back, he would he done it already, or at least called or had that stupid agency tell us or something." answered Heath.

"Maybe, but I want him back." Katie said sadly. They momentarily held and squeezed each other's hands in the sisters' unspoken code, then let go. And with that, silence fell and they went off to sleep.

Meanwhile, Moca was trying to get comfortable in these new surroundings. The bunk was comfortable and large; maybe too large. Of course she still missed lying against her husband and would never again like sleeping alone. They would go to sleep intertwined like spoons in a drawer, then spread out later, but one always touching the other throughout the night. "Coming from inland, and never having even seen the actual oceans, here I am, an Indian girl sleeping on a ship; floating in the night!" Moca thought. Doubts always had crept into her psyche just before sleep. "Is this all worth it?" she thought, "Should we have just stayed in Kansas on safe dry land? But then, there is drought and tornadoes. She was set not to be pitiful, but it was a hard inner life for her without Sam. The farm in Kansas had ceased to be very profitable and this new life was a new chance. Does not everything bring its own risks and rewards?"

Then, as she would dispel the doubts, the next phase just before sleep would be the dream-vision phase that would slip in automatically of their own creative volition; sometimes strange, sometimes containing a foretelling or warning, or a symbolic point of view about a past situation. And sometime, something completely unexplainable. Moca would always verbalize these to Sam just after they happened as a last thing before sleep, but now there was no one to whisper and tell of the dream visions. But tonight that seemed to bypass, and, starting to gain a measure of comfort, she drifted off listening to wavelets lap against the hull.

CHAPTER 10

HOME PORT

"Look at that!" Said Moca. "The porpoises are playing with us!" As the *Tradewind* took off from the pier and began making way, the porpoises came along and started following the boat. The plan was to depart early and travel the Ship Channel up to upper Galveston Bay and enter the channel into Clear Lake. That should put them there in about 6 hours, or easily by noon.

The crew put up a simple small sail on the front of the boat, called a jib, and then hoisted the mainsail on the mast and boom. All the while, Captain "B" left the engine running. "This called motor-sailing." Said Captain "B" as if narrating a film. "Best to motor-sail in channels for navigation reasons."

Jon took all this in, and said, "Capt'n "B", what happens when we turn up here in a minute, or if the wind shifts?" He was thinking ahead, beginning to think like a Captain should.

"We'll just make an adjustment." Said "B" "We'll want to keep the wind, no matter where it comes from, striking the sail at about the same angle. If the wind is within about twenty degrees either side of the front, we'll take down the sail; otherwise we just trim the sail to catch the wind, and help push the boat along, with the engine running. My job or at least one of my jobs is to keep the helm calm and going the right way, and watch of for objects, and an eye of the depth sounder here." he said laying a hand on the device. The channel was dredged to a standard depth of forty-five feet in the middle. "B" preferred to travel on the right side of the channel holding about thirty-five feet. So watching channel markers and depth gauge gave him pretty good guidance information. "Navigation is about confirming your position multiple ways, and having those ways agree." Captain "B" wrapped up, "And each way should be independent of the others."

Jon thought carefully, and asked "What are our ways right now, Capt'n "B"?"

Captain "B" replied, "The chart, the marker ahead, the marker behind, and the depth gauge. The compass also, I guess, although I don't rely on them in channels."

Jon considered what Captain "B" had been saying, and thought, there's going to be a lot to this navigation stuff.

They made the turn out of the Galveston Ship Channel up into the main Houston Ship Channel otherwise known as HSC and went by Day Marker 25. They were well on the way.

Captain "B" said, "It's pretty much a straight shot from here, up to just past Red Fish Reef, where we turn out of the HSC and head straight to the Clear Lake channel entrance."

Jon agreed. He had reviewed the charts for this part of the trip, and had most of it committed to memory by now. The Reef was actually an oyster-shell spoil bank right on the left side of the HDC going north. It was common to see pleasure boats anchoring on the west side of the reef since it made a kind of protected cove for anchoring overnight. It was a popular end point destination for the sailboat crowd, and there weren't many destinations.

It was now ten thirty and they were making great time.

Jon saw something ahead that looked like an exposed reef, that also had some low trees and bushes on it, and that was Red Fish Reef. The Channel dog legged to the left around the reef and just past the oyster-shell island; they tacked out of the channel and headed to Clear Lake. They had to cross Upper Galveston Bay to get there, and it was about eight miles. It was a glorious and sunny Saturday about eleven o'clock and the bay was full of pleasure boats out enjoying the day. The *Tradewind* was bigger and had a salty sea-going look about her and attracted the attention of almost every boat that passed. As Marker Two, the outer Clear Lake channel marker approached, they took down all sails and motored down the straight channel, until they entered land and motored past restaurants, boardwalk, rides like Ferris wheels and the like and marinas where thousands of boats were parked. The little town of Kemah was on the left and Seabrook of the right. The Highway 146 Kemah Bridge loomed ahead. The bridge was a hugh, high, six lane affair, and was fairly new, replacing a very very old swing drawbridge affair that was a real mess and in no way could keep up with the growth of the area. The "Lake" had been a sleepy little place for many years, but the first thing to happen was NASA being located there. Then Houston's expansion was legendary and taking on gigantic proportions and it was now Clear Lake's turn in the breech. Houston was home to the nation's space program, oil field equipment and engineering companies, drilling operations, corporate headquarters to major oil companies, shipping and transportation hub, and many other enterprises. It was now the third largest city and metropolitan area in the United States.

Tradewind travelled the short distance through the entrance to the "Lake" and then broke out into the "Lake" itself, which was not to large. They had to stay strictly in the channel since the "Lake" was very shallow. Even "B" was impressed at all the activity. Safe Shore Harbour, *Tradewind's* new home, was at the far end of the "Lake" and soon enough they were almost there. The boat turned a shape left and entered the Safe Shore Harbour channel, which was sharp and marked be a fake lighthouse. Soon they saw a nice marina filled with thousands of boats. Their spot was Pier 3 Slip 33 odd numbered slips in the right side of the pier and even on the left. They turned slowly down the channel and found their slip.

Captain "B" deftly guided the *Tradewind* into its slip as the crewmen leaped off, tying down the dock lines and making things neat, on and off the boat. The slip next door had a very salty looking fine sailboat with a fellow poking his head out of the hatchway taking on the arrival of his new neighbor. "Hi there." he said to "B" "Great looking boat." said the fellow.

Later on, Jon and Moca were down on the dock walk way, and introduced themselves to the next door neighbor, Bob, who was now comfortably sitting in the cockpit of his fine sailboat. They found him to pleasant and knowledgeable; a single guy in full bachelor mode, very interested in sailing. Bob was born in the central states, but had worked in Houston for many years, and had a house north of town. It took him about an hour to commute down to his boat from home, and in fact he more or less live on his boat about half the time since he had a lot of customers in that Clear Lake area.

CHAPTER 11

LIVE ABOARD

Several weeks had past and life aboard the boat was settling down to a routine. They all were all getting used to the coziness of the ship's interior. The hull's shape dictated the outer limits of their living space. Not flat and rectangular like the slab of a house but curved and streamlined to meet the needs of a ship whose natural place is underway at sea. The hull's outer shape needs determined their inner quarters and it wasn't always level or spacious, but it all seemed natural and right, considering.

Jon stood in the companionway halfway out and looked over to see slip-mate Bob polishing the funnel-looking things, which were bronze dorade vent cowlings on the *Dama*. *Tradewind* and much smaller *Dama Du Mar* were the saltiest boats on the pier. It was common to see people stop and talk about the two boats.

"Hey bud," said the distracted Bob, looking back down to his task, "what's up?"

"I going over to Captain Bill's at Y.E.S. Need some stuff. You know how it is, a boats a hole in the water in which to pour money, as they say. Do you need anything?"

"No but thanks," laughed Bob, who was still working, "When are you guys gonna take her out the first time?"

Eileen, Bob's girlfriend of the week, stepped out from below, bringing a glass of sun tea. It was already brewing hot in the Texas sun. Bob had erected sun shades that covered the entire deck of the *Dama* giving it a nice tropical look and was very functional. "Here hon, just made it. Drink that and I'll get you some more," said Eileen.

Jon jumped off the boat and headed up to the car, answering "Next week is the plan. Have a lot to do though. See you later."

Yacht Equipment Specialties was just around the lake across the Kemah drawbridge. It was always an adventure to go in there. The place was full of historical looking ship's gear and supplies. It had the look and feel of an old time hardware store. The gruff Captain Bill knew where everything was. Bill would sit on his stool by a messy table piled high with invoices and receipts near the center of the store. The transaction counter and cash register were not far away but in a separate area where his employees handled the ringing up of sales and fielding other questions. But if you needed something unusual or requiring related knowledge, Captain Bill was the man.

"Hey Captain Bill," Jon hailed as he walked in."

The Y.E.S. parrot blurted "Hi Captain Bill, Hello! Hello!" Max, the parrot was a store fixture and his cage was moved around from time to time in the store. Max's' large cage was usually either up by the front foyer as you came in the store, or back by plumbing, but in any case, he was a special attraction and enjoyed the constant stream of customers and kids that always stopped to play with the beautiful bird.

Jon asked "How old is the bird?"

Bill replied "Who in the world knows? Maybe about

twenty?! The rotten old cuss." he joked with affection to the bird, handing him a cracker from behind his register.

Jon headed to the stairway to go up to the second floor of the store to look at rain gear. Upstairs looked like it used to be a bar or a club of some kind. It had a bar and stools, plus rubber dinghies, rain gear, shoes and boots, and other store that didn't go on the ground floor. It was dark and most of the lights up there were off. It was also hot up there.

CHAPTER 12

THE MAP OF TREASURE BAY

"Look at that!" said Jon. It was a very old piece of wrinkled paper, folded crisply into several layers. He was afraid it would tear as he slowly unfolded the old map, but it was stronger than he thought. The paper seemed thicker than normal, kind of like a paper sack. It was obviously a map, but of what?

The map was stuck deep inside an old dusty bronze diving helmet that was beneath a stack of foul weather gear. From the looks, nobody had disturbed the stack for years. It was on the second floor of "Y.E.S." yacht store, and few customers ever came up there. Who knew where in the world Captain Bill got some of his oddball merchandise in that store. Jon slide the heavy helmet along the floor from underneath the stack of clothing, and it was heavy. What made him turn it over and peer inside, other than pure curiosity?

Yet, right there in his hand was an ancient folded paper document; it was a hand drawn old map. It looked like rivers and creeks, a couple of paths or roads, none of which had names. He twisted and turned the paper trying to get bearings; There was an "N" with a circle and arrow on the sheet, so there was North. "It all looked kind of familiar." Jon told Moca. "I think I've seen that pattern before, so we'll see." He folded and tucked the map into his pants carefully, and they left the store.

Back at the boat, Jon got out his charts and the old map, and he started comparing. In not too long, he thought he had a likely candidate place to travel and dig. He had ask Lantana to do some research on the famous pirate and privateer, Jean Lafitte, who had operated along the Gulf Coast between Galveston, Texas and New Orleans, Louisiana in the first part of the eighteen-hundreds.

Lantana said to Jon, "Little brother, if you are going searching for gold and treasure, please be careful. You'll have our whole family with you, don't forget."

"Yes, Lan. That is certainly something to think about. You just do well in college, OK?"

CHAPTER 13

QUEST FOR GOLD

J on was not positively sure if the map covered Lake Charles,
or Beaumont, since there were no town names, roads or
man-made waterways at the time Lafitte had drawn his
map. "Momma, we're going to have to explore around Lake
Charles a little to see if the map applies to that Calcasieu
River there, or the Neches River in Beaumont."

There were several smaller sloughs and creeks off the
Calcasieu River, but none looked exactly like the Lafitte
map Jon had. Owing to the difference in times and no
familiar names on the map, Jon had only rough shapes to
go by. Plus, modernization and bridges and roads confused
things greatly. One looked likely, whose modern name was
Contraband Bayou which ran off Calcasieu Lake and River.
However it didn't seem long enough plus had a nice housing
neighborhood on the banks. Most houses there had private
piers; they could not go digging around. The map showed
kind of a hill or high spot and they did not see that on their
maps.

The Sabine River above Orange, Texas had a long slough,
called Cow Bayou, but it went the wrong way. The only other

was off the Neches River just a little north of the I-10 bridge and Beaumont. That had to be it.

The West's did not hang around Lake Charles for long and continued westward on the ICW, bypassing Orange altogether, and turned out of the ICW and went up the Neches River to Beaumont, Texas. They would anchor the *Tradewind* opposite downtown, get into the small tender-boat, and go find search the next day. Jon knew about a band of people that lived on that river up north of town, called Caneyheads, and they did not sound like folks they wanted to deal with. Even locals didn't go in there. Nobody knew much about them, except the rumors about inbreeding and criminals, etc.

It was even said that a Bigfoot was known to live in the Big Thicket woods that surrounded the lower Neches River. It was a pretty spooky place, indeed.

CHAPTER 14

A PARTIAL FIND

In the small boat going up the Neches River outside of Beaumont, Texas, they motored against the weak, hardly noticeable current. They went under the I-10 Bridge, past the Beaumont Boat club and then twisted and turned following the wide river. The Beaumont Country Club was up north on the river, but Ten Mile Slough was only about one-half way up, about three miles. It would be on the right, and not mark be either sigh nor landmark. But Jon was sure the prize would be up this slough, based on his map.

Jon said to "B", "Let's keep bearing to the right, best you can. Should be around the next bend." He was getting very excited. In the older days, it was common to see people water skiing and a lot of pleasure boats on the river, but now so much anymore. Hardly anyone fished the river. In very old days, logs were floated down the river, and a few cotton barges pushed by steamboats.

Soon, they rounded the bend in the river, and Jon saw the slough up ahead. It was hard to see, and looked like a cutaway in the bank, more than a navigable slough. After entering the cutout in the river's bank, the slough turn right for a while, then began its' snaking and twisting for a while, with nothing but swamp on either side. The map was following well, so far. It showed the banks becoming solid ground in about another mile and a small hill on the left bank. Jon was pointing along their route with his finger, as Moca looked on, both, looking at the map and looking at the scenery as they went. It had not taken them long to get up here from Beaumont, so *they had plenty of time*, she thought, *depending on how much digging they might have to do.*

Jon told "B", "Pull up hard on the bank just up there on the left by that big tree."

As the nose of the boat rode up on dry land, Jon and Moca leaped out and tied up the boat to a tree, while Captain "B" turned off the engine. Jon and Moca were ahead, already scouting out the map's directions.

"Y'all slow down and watch out for gators and snakes." Said "B" picking up a bit of the southern accent. They walked through some high grass for a little ways, toward the top of the hill, then, there it was; They were over the spot one the map. They could tell by the hollow "clunk" type sound their boots made as they walked over the spot. "It seems to be a pit covered by planks." Said Captain "B".

Jon and Moca were already on each side trying to fit their shovels under a plank to lift it up, which they were doing handily. Soon they had removed about ten planks, exposing about ten more going the other way, in criss cross fashion.

Once all the planks were up, they were looking at some number of wooden boxes, double stacked. "Let's lift this first on out and see what's inside." Said Moca, looking carefully all around to make sure no one, or no creature, was sneaking up on them. "This place is about as wild and strange as anything I've ever seen in my life." She could not get the thought of those Caneyhead people that lived in the deep woods somewhere around here. Or a Bigfoot.

Jon and "B" carefully lifted the first crate out, and it was extremely heavy. They beat off the lock with a hammer and chisel that Jon had thought to bring, swung open the lid, and they all gasped. Gold!

On the way back to the *Tradewind*, the little boat rode heavy in the water, but they were travelling with the current. It was getting dark and mosquitoes were coming out. They pulled up to the waiting ship and tied extra lines to help load the heavy cargo.

Carefully, they got it all done and decided to wait out the dawn then leave for home, all down the ICW. Still it was quite aways back down the Neches to Port Arthur then via the ICW to Galveston then back up the HSC to Clear Lake.

Jon crawled into his bunk and was comfortably think about how wealthy he had now become, even splitting up the fortune fairly with "B" and his mom. They would all be comfortable with their shares. He was anxious to get back to Clear Lake.

At dawn, Captain and crew all came topsides and began to make ready. Some Beaumont radio and newspaper reporters were gathering on shore, since *Tradewind* was beginning to attract attention, Jon gave a quick interview, but without mentioning anything about the treasure find. He had decided to save that for Houston and later. He did not want to reveal anything about the treasure, especially at this time, with so many miles to cover.

CHAPTER 15

QUINTANA

Jon was hanging out on the dock messing around the boat, and happened to glance over towards the fuel dock past pier 1 just in time to see an older fishing boat pull up for fuel. Even at this distance he saw a girl with long dark hair step off to help tie up the old boat. It looked like it was the father at the helm and probably some brothers or cousins as crew. It was unusual to see such an older boat in the marina, since it was an upper-end type facility, near the fancy hotel and all. The older craft seemed interesting but out of place. Plus, that girl looked great and he was on his way over on the pretense to buy a Coke or something.

Halfway there, he looked up to see the girl walking towards him. Slowing, he said, "Hello", then abruptly stopped.

The girl looked Jon squarely in the face and said, "Hey you. I saw you over on your pier when we were coming in. Were you coming to see me?"

"Well, I ... "Jon started, kind of smiling and looking downward.

"Don't worry, I was walking over here to see you." she said smiling. "Anyway, I like to walk around and look at all the fancy big boats when we come over here, which isn't often. Are you all new here?"

He didn't know where to start. "Well, kind of came down from Kansas, and ..."

The girl said, "We came over from Double Bayou, a small fishing village across the bay. My uncle has a shrimping tag for the channel over here and he can't use it right now, so he lets my Pappa use it. We are shrimping and getting some good ones today. You can come do a run with us, but we'll have to drop you off up by the bridge, unless you want to go all the way back with us. My name is Quintana Andros." Feigning embarrassment, she went on, "My dad is Greek, originally from Galveston. Momma's Spanish."

Jon could hardly think. The girl was stunning close up. He was almost breathless. Lean and fit, large dark eyes, with long black hair that glistened in the sun, brown smooth skin tanned even more. She wore blue jean cutoffs that revealed her beautiful muscular legs and gorgeous bare feet. He was totally awe-struck. He finally managed, "Uh, I'm Jon West, and we just moved aboard our boat, the *Tradewind* over there." pointing back to pier 3. "I'd really like to go try shrimping, but I better let them know, so they can come pick me up. Come with me real quick so I can ask." He turned and she followed. Instinctively, he felt an urge to reach out for her hand, but stuffed into his pocket instead. The girl noticed and softly chuckled.

Walking up to the boat, Moca was out on the deck lounging and reading and saw Jon approaching with the girl. Moca was reclining in a deck chair with a big sun hat on and sunglasses. Actually she had been watching the entire transaction over her book. Quick introductions were made, and then Moca lowered her glasses and peered over them for a moment assessing the girl, and then said, "OK Jon, I'll drive over to Double Bayou to pick you up. Quintana, is five hours from now enough time?"

"Yes ma'am, just make it nine o'clock and that's plenty of time. I'll fix something to eat for y'all. It's a small place, just ask at the store where the Andros place is.. its close and you won't miss it." And it was done, and as the two walked back up the pier, Moca had a warm good feeling, for some reason. "Are you sure this is going to be ok with your father?" Jon said. "I'm sure." replied Quintana.

After introductions, Jon was aboard the old shrimp boat, and was underway out of the marina to shrimp, and then head back all the way across the bay. It wasn't long before they were in the Clear Creek channel and the boat slowed and the crew of uncles prepared to drop the boards, which meant drop the shrimp-net and start another drag which they did. Jon stayed out of the way, but watched intently.

"This is the boring part", said Quintana. "Let's sit down over here and talk. Tell me about Kansas."

Over the next while, they talked of themselves, their families, schools, interests, music, and the things that young adults talked about. Near the end of the first shrimp drag the two had scooted closer together to talk more comfortably over the loud drone of the shrimp boats diesel engine. Several times he had to lean even closer to talk, and had accidentally brushed face lips against her beautiful hair, and noticed how soft it felt and how sweet she smelled.

The boat slowed and an uncle went over to the hoist controls and pulled a hydraulic lever to begin raising the net. It took a while. Finally the dripping net was hauled aboard and sure enough the pocket of the net was full of flapping tails. The net dumped out on the freshly watered down culling tray and the work began. Everybody began telling Jon what to do, but in a happy excited way, not a bad way. A full net was a happy event. Some things went overboard, some shrimp were left alone and put whole in one of several five gallon plastic buckets, and others of a certain size were headed live on the spot and put into other containers. There were lots of interesting other creatures, Jon noticed, even a gross ugly eel, which was snapped whip-like by a gloved-handed uncle Paul, then tossed it over. "Good for nothin', yeah." he said.

Jon and Quintana were stationed next to each other, now working together in a nice rhythm. The rhythm seemed to magnify each other's work. It was like they were communicating without talking. He felt it. She must have. Every once in a while they would catch each other's eye and it seemed to linger a little longer each time. The next drag had already started as they finished the culling, and hands and arms were sprayed off. She playfully sprayed him with the hose, but it was hot and felt good. They went and stood on the bow for a while and together looked out on the bay.

"See way over there, way past the ship channel. That's where I live. We'll be heading back across probably after this next drag," Quintana said, and added, "It's been a good day, I know my Dad's happy with the catch. It's how we live you know. I'm glad I came out today, I started not to."

"Quintana," Jon said as they turned to look into each other's eyes, "I'm so glad we met today." And then with nothing more to be said, their gaze lingered quietly in the warm bay breeze. He reached for her hand and hers found his. Finally each leaned in and their lips softly met for more than a moment this first time.

<hr/>

It was as if time had ceased, but the old shrimp boat was well past the ship channel and almost across Trinity Bay. The entrance to the long Double Bayou channel was just ahead.

They were running a little late and Moca had already arrived, and found the Andros house and was waiting patiently on the dock. As she saw the boat coming to dock, she immediately knew something was different with Jon. The way he stood on the deck, the way he moved in relation to the girl, the way they moved together. A rhythm was already being established between the two, the way you instinctively know when two people are a couple and not just two individuals. So this is it, she thought, and she was glad and warm in the heart for her son, for both of them actually, because she really liked Quintana already.

"Hi Mrs. West." shouted Quintana. Jon waved and smiled. As the boat docked and the uncles jumped off to tie up, Quintana was first off, with Jon on the boat holding a steadying hand for Quintana, as she held on and helped him balance off to the dock. The two ran up excited, and told of the catch and the trip. Papa Andros came up and introduced himself to Moca and they all went inside while the uncles put away the catch into the tanks and coolers that were on property. "Let's go up and have a drink and get something to eat, how about it?" said Papa Andros in a very gregarious mood. "Did you meet Mrs Andros yet? Come on, let's go up."

Mrs. Andros was Hispanic and also very pretty. Not hard to see where Quintana got her looks in this beautiful family, thought Moca.

The screen door flapped as Mrs. Andros already had pappas cold bottle of Ouzo and a second bottle without alcohol, out on the table and five small jigger glasses ready. Moca guessed that he planned to serve the kids too, so it must be ok and customary around here. She knew Ouzo was Greek alcoholic liquor, but had never had any. It was a cloudy drink, and tasted somewhat like liquorish .. "yuk" she thought, but drank it to be social. The group was very social and happy. The whole house had good vibrations, Moca thought.

Aside privately, Quintana asked Jon if he had ever had

Ouzo before. "No. Had a few beers on the farm during high school. After haying in the hot summer, we would stack hay in the barn and it would get so hot, we were allowed to have a six pack to share among us and nothing tasted better than those beers! But no, never any hard liquor of any kind, except a sip at family Christmas gatherings and such. Enough to know I didn't like it; but this stuff kind of grows on you. It's better after the first jigger. It doesn't even taste like liquorish anymore." She touched his hand under the table each time they talked.

Moca and Mama and Papa Andros were busy chatting about family and recipes, and histories. She learned that Mama was actually Castilian Spanish and had come directly from Spain. There was actually Royalty in her background, but Moca couldn't follow the details through Mama's accent. Papa Andros parents had come to Galveston from the old country, and had worked in the maritime industry. Papa Andros had retired early from a petrochemical plant, and shrimped for a retirement second career. They actually did quite well it sounded and were not simply poor fisher people. They had chosen this lifestyle and had chosen simplicity and happiness. How lucky for Mama, Moca thought, that Papa Andros had not chosen to go off on strange foreign clandestine adventures and disappear like her husband Sam West had. How she missed him, and the hour or the drink made her miss him so much more right at this moment. She broke down a little, while telling some of this to Mama Andros, who put her arms around Moca in comfort. Papa Andros came back in the room and livened up the pace saying loudly, "come on now girls, perk up! No down in the dumps hereabouts. Mama fill the jiggers with more ouzo, and I'm putting on some music." And pretty soon they were all up dancing.

"Look at that! Mom, I didn't know you could dance that good." Jon said.

"You should have seen me and your Dad! We cut a rug as they say."

In a minute, Quintana grabbed Jon and started trying to show him some swing dance steps, but maybe he had too much Ouzo, or was just too muddled in the day's events to do it very well. Quintana took it in stride, and as a slow song came on, the two naturally move into closed position and moved together as one.

None of this had escaped Papa or Mama Andros. Quintana had never brought a boy around before. She was a smart and beautiful daughter. She made the best grades and never disappointed the family in the slightest way. Mother and daughter had had many long talks of boys and men and relationships and life. There was nothing left unsaid between them and Mama knew Quintana was well prepared to enjoy life, and also for her next steps in life. She was capable and they trusted her judgement completely.

The slow music played and Jon felt her sway to the beat and it had never been better. "I might like this dancing thing." he whispered, as he nuzzled her soft hair and found her ear. She pressed against his face and turned her head slowly, maintaining constant contact and found his lips for the second time this day. Jon was completely enveloped in the moment and in Quintana's being.

Moca's laughing voice came through, saying, "Break it up you two. Jon, we have to go, now. It's getting late and we have a drive."

Going downstairs, they all said goodbyes, Moca got into the car and Mama and Papa Andros vanished back upstairs, leaving the two to say goodbyes. All the adults seem to understand the two would need a little extra time and some privacy.

"Quintana," Jon said holding her directly in front of him, "when this day began, none of us had any clue of each other or how this day would turn out. It's been one of the best days of my life. I want you to know how I feel." he said as he looked straight into her eyes. He had their hands over her heart, between them.

"I did." she softly responded. "I had a dream last night and I felt a good warmth right where our hands are right now. I knew something good was coming today. That's why I almost didn't go with Papa, afraid I would miss something here, but see, you never know where or when you'll find your fate. Jon ..."

"Shhh .. Quintana, I'll be right across that bay, and be with you in here." and they kissed and explored each other to make the memory last. As hunger grew in both of them, they pushed away, he backed to the already started car, and off they went.

—————

Nothing was said in the car for quite a while. Finally Moca said, "Jon, you'll have to drive, I'm getting very sleepy."

"OK Mom, pull over. I'm wide awake." Jon said, still energized in a very rosy glow.

"I'm certain you are, son." chuckled Moca, as they changed seats and drove on. She was quickly asleep, but Jon listened to the late-night radio and thought of Quintana and the day's events with each stripe of the highway.

CHAPTER 16

THE STORE

J on and Moca parked the car and walked across the very hot asphalt parking lot, and on into the interesting looking building. It seemed to have two stories, and one narrow tunnelled entrance, busy with all types of nautical junk propped up, hanging, and setting about for sale. Straight through inside, there was a glass display counter area and at the end, there sat Captain Bill, owner of Y.E.S. Yacht Equipment Speciality store. Just on the other side of the aisle was a giant iron parrot cage with a beautiful like parrot inside, saying parrot words one would expect. To proceed on into the main parts of the store, you had to pass by and receive a greeting from gruff Captain Bill and also the parrot.

"Hey there Skip," Said Bill to Jon, with a nod but no words to Moca. Bill was a man's man. He sat there behind his cash register, presiding over his property like a big old heavy set frog, bumpy complexion, black combed-back hair, big black glasses and gruff deep booming voice. You could tell this store was crammed from floor to ceiling with serious yacht stuff from every age and stage, every manufacturer sail, power, and other, all hand selected by Bill himself. This was a chandlery unequalled anywhere, even up east.

Jon was amazed at all the stuff in the store, and just walk slowly, look carefully at all the goods. There was a second floor, too. It was like a big magic store except dedicated to sailing stuff. Bill and his parrot had been perfectly sent from Central Casting.

Back at the boat, Job asked Capt'n "B" if he'd been over to the yacht store yet. "Yes, it's an amazing place, for sure. Hold your wallet when you go in there. I've seen some great chandleries, but Captain Bill is one of the best I've seen.

Jon said, "I opened an account there, so if there anything you see that we need, just go for it."

"Ok, I'll do just that." said "B". "I know for sure we need two more anchor rigs. You know Boy, there's a lot to anchoring technology that I need to show you, and the best was is to rig up a complete anchor rig from the start. When you set anchor in your boat, out in some strange waters, in the dark of maybe a stormy night, you will need to weather a gale and strong conditions and your life and safety of the ship will depend on the lowly anchor." Capt'n "B" continued, "First, how deep is the water you're in. Let out five times that depth in anchor line, called Rode."

Jon loved this. Learning something this valuable from an experienced Captain like Capt'n "B" was priceless, and he was relishing the moment.

"Then, the Rode needs to be strong strand nylon braided cord at least three-quarters inch thick. Then weave on a galvanized steel thimble and put on a galvanized matching fitting to attach to the anchor chain. Secure the screw of the fitting with stainless wire so it can't come undone. The chain should be what is referred to as "proof" chain guaranteeing the minimum strength of the chain. The length of chain on a pleasure boat anchor rig should be at least as long as the length of the boat itself. A fifty foot craft needs a fifty foot chain."

Jon nodded, taking it all in, in minute detail.

"Since the chain is heavy, it lays along the bottom causing a favorable angle and shock absorber effect to the bobbing of the ship floating on a rough sea above. Finally, you'll need another Galvanized fitting fastening the chain to the anchor. There's great argument about the best type of anchor. Some of that depends on the exact nature of the bottom itself. Rock, mud, sand, shell or whatever. My choice in mud or sand is the 45 pound Bruce anchor. Hard to go wrong with one of those. But, there are all kinds of different anchors to choose from. When you go to set the anchor, you back the boat under power to cause the anchor to plow into the bottom. It can dig very deep and you almost can't get it out when you're ready to leave. There are occasions where you'll want to put out a stern anchor also, and that's lesson for another day.

Jon was amazed at "B"s depth and breadth of knowledge. There was so much to know.

Wrapping up, "B" said, "Also, the most important thing is, an anchor rig is a linear system, not parallel; the whole things is only as strong as the weakest link. Remember that lad; no weak links at all; ever."

CHAPTER 17

PREPARING FOR THE GULF

C aptain "B" knew this first trip offshore would be primarily a training and break-in trip for the new owners. He thought he would go a little more extravagant on the ship's food for the trip. Not exactly that he normally fed the crew hardtack and water, but not a king's feast either. And the ship had plenty of storage anyway. He was compiling a very long and detailed grocery shopping list.

Meanwhile, the crew was working on another list of ships items and repairs that needed to be done before sailing. Crewman Claude Bergeron was working the engine area and was changing the oil, and checking the ship's batteries water levels. He actually checked and inspected the banks of the huge batteries twice just to be sure since running out of electrical power at the wrong time could be catastrophic. After that, he checked the bilge for any signs of leakage, and then the operation of the bilge pumps and their automatic float switches that would take care of any rising water in the bilge. The bilge is the lowest area of the boat and any incoming water or leaks collect there. A lot of ships troubles show up in the bilge first. The bilge pump transfers the water back overboard. "B" handed the food supplies list to Slim for his additions and comments.

Slim perused a minute, then said, "Capt'n "B"? What about we add some dried beans, olive oil and butter. I think we're low on black pepper too."

"Fine, write it down." Capt'n "B" replied. "In fact, I'm going to send you to the store, and you just get anything we forgot. Don't want to be caught short for the new folks".

"Rog. Capt'n." said Slim affirmatively as he folded up the list and stuffed it in his pocket.

Katie and Heather were lying on the salon couch playing Slam and one of them said, "Mr. Slim, do we have to eat broccoli at sea? Can we not? Can you not cook any, please!?"

"I'll take that under consideration, there missy ma'am!" smiled Slim, "Not partial to it either."

"You missy Maam's shouldn't be too particular!" growled "B" as he went up the companionway steps. He ducked in his head and glanced around the main cabin once more for anything loose that would go rogue in a rough sea, and flashed a departing smile at the girls.

Although the *Tradewind* was primarily an island trading cargo vessel back in the South Pacific, numerous times they had carried extra passengers for hire, and Slim was used to provisioning for extra mouths. Captain Pete had even made a deal with a travel agency for a while to carry vacationers. The crew pretty much hated that phase. They got so tired of hearing the vacationing landlubbers saying the same dumb things, asking the same questions, and generally being lazy deck lumps and constantly eating and stuffing themselves, and generally doing weird things on the boat. This was partly how Slim knew easy meals and goodies that made non-sailors happy, and, kind of like the cruise lines know, lots of good food aboard makes for a happy ship.

Capt'n "B" and the family had arranged to have a

scheduled meeting aboard ship to have a final and formal "prep class" on what to do and not to do on the first little trip out tomorrow. All were convening in the main salon for the gathering. "Shall we come to order, mates?" Said "B" trying to be officious. First thing is to obey the Captain and ask question later. There are times when I or the crew will be very busy and communication will be terse, so please don't take offense. Anything we tell you is for a reason and it'll be a darn good one. Can't predict everything that might come up, so we'll leave it at that; just follow orders, and be quick about it. Second, we're here to learn and experience, so be observant and ask a lot of questions when time allows. Scoop up after yourselves and no stuff laying around. Try to stay above decks; if you go below, you're going to be hit by the sea-sick, until you get used to it. Has to do with not seeing the horizon. And you kids try not to be bouncing all over the ship, especially on deck; try to stick in one place for a while. Keep one hand for yourself, and one for the ship, that means be holding on to something all the time. More people are tossed overboard when a sudden wave pitches the ship, even a big one like this, and even bigger. You can get hurt easy, and you won't see it coming. Don't wrap any lines around your hands like this," and "B" demonstrated. "Do it over handed like this, lest ye get a lost hand or fingers.".

Katie and Heather grimaced and looked at Momma, who told them to look back at "B" and pay attention.

"B" went on, "That's about it for now. Any questions? If not, we'll be leaving dock before first light, that means we pull out and throw the lines at 4:30 am sharp, so every get a good night's bunk. Slim will fix us a breakfast after dawn while we're underway. Good night all." and with that "B" disappeared to his cabin.

Jon scooted over next to Fred Bergeron who was studying the charts for the trip. Fred said, "We'll be seeing some of my territory, over there at Vermillion Bay. Louisiana bound we are. It'll be good to see it. Sho' will".

The chart had a lot of little numbers regularly spaced all over the blue part of the chart, which marked the Gulf. "Fred, what are these numbers?" Jon asked.

"Those are water soundings - depths - indicated in feet on this chart, in fathoms on others. A fathom is six feet." replied Fred. "Can't make a mistake about that. Always know which you be a'lookin' at, lest you might run aground. You thinking fathoms, but it's feet and all-a-sudden you're in the mud or on the rocks."

"I get it." said Jon, feeling over-taught. "I noticed it's really shallow out there off the Louisiana coast. Whole lot of offshore oil rigs too."

Fred said, "See that shipping lane, we'll be travelling on the edge of that. Should be a little better sailing a little further out. See, there's where we'll turn into the Vermilion Bay channel. We'll go in, camp out one night somewhere, maybe anchored out, the head back the next day. Two or three day trip the first time out is plenty."

Jon wondered what Fred meant by "plenty" but didn't ask.

———◦———

Jon was finally comfortably in his bunk with the light off, and was daydreaming into sleep. He thought about Quintana, and how she was happily going about her business, helping around the house, and hopefully thinking of him. He wished she were here more, but right now, his main direction was getting familiar with the boat and the upcoming trip.

CHAPTER 18

DEPARTURE

Predawn came early, as Jon climbed out of his bunk and hit the deck at 4:30 am. Captain "B" was listening to NOA Weather radio on the VHF while examining some nautical charts of the area they were going. A few heavy morning clouds loomed among the smaller ones, but it looked like a promising day. Maybe just a passing shower or two but an otherwise typical gulf coast summers day.

"Anything to worry about?" checked Jon.

"Nie," Said "B", "A fine day she be."

Jon sat down on the deck locker box, still wiping away sleep. The engine was running and the crew walked up carrying their fresh coffee and untied the dock lines and Capt'n "B" slid behind the helm and eased the big sailboat away from the dock as the crew hopped on. And they were off, just like that!

———⊰●⊱———

Heather and Katie appeared out of the companionway like to anxious little squirrels, already jabbering about the goings on. Their little heads were turning here and there

DON A. LACKEY

looking at the other shipping traffic in already busy in the Galveston Ship Channel.

"Jon, what is that?" asked Heather point at a very loud funny looking boat passing them.

"That's a crew-boat going out to an oil rig." replied Jon. The crew boats carried drill long drill pipe, and other people and supplies to and from the many and distant offshore drilling platforms which cluttered offshore Texas and Louisiana. They had very powerful diesel engines and were indeed loud. There were also shrimp boats, a large tanker heading up the Houston ship channel and push boats with barges, and of course one of the five ever present Bolivar-Galveston ferries.

Jon frequently watched "B's" face and demeanor as the were underway. He knew soon enough that he would be behind the helm. Jon noticed the relaxed but vigilant Captain "B" gazed far out in the distance lot, with occasional glances mostly at the depth finder instrument. About once a minute "B" would scan port and starboard, and astern for quick traffic checks.

"Look y'all" Katie exclaimed pointing east, "I can almost see the Sun!". The crew had already belayed the dock lines and were on the foredeck automatically keeping watch and relaxing. Claude Bergeron was on the back deck smoking a cigarette and gazed back at Galveston. He had been enjoying the town and especially going out to the Strand clubs at night and listening to live bands and live ladies, something the south seas were often short of.

The *Tradewind* was going fine past the Galveston-side ferry landing and Coast Guard base and rounding to starboard missing most of the famous Bolivar Roads, one of the busiest crossings of any maritime channels in the world, by vessel count or tonnage, and almost any other measure one could think of. A push boat carrying two doubles (barges) full of petrochemicals was just pushing out from the Bolivar ICW, turning north to go up towards Houston to one the many petrochemical plants up along the Houston Ship Channel. The amount of barge traffic between Freeport, Texas, and New Orleans was immense. Push boats with barge tows, went slow and careful, and it was amazing how few accidents there were. They mostly carried crude oil, intermediate products and feed stocks for plastic production, and other finished products like diesel and bunker fuel, jet fuel, and gasoline. The Intracoastal Waterway, known as the ICW or "ditch" was their main water highway. The creation of the Intracoastal Waterway was authorized by the U.S. Congress in 1919 and is maintained by the U.S. Corp of Engineers. Federal law provides for the waterway to be maintained at a hundred feet wide and a minimum depth of 12 feet, which has changed over the years.

There was a lot to see. Some porpoises were joining them frolicking and surfacing around the boat. A lot of smaller fishing boats were already positioned around their favorite spots, or heading toward them with anxious speed. Other sailboats were heading out as well. Bolivar Roads around Galveston was a busy place.

They continued out the jetties, which pretty much ran eastward, the direction *Tradewind* was heading anyway to Louisiana, on this trip at least. As boat rounded the end of the jetties, the morning winds had stiffened a little, an effect that happens most summer mornings because of the night-to-day temperature differences between land and see in the area. Also, Jon could feel it getting more rough, with what seemed like more serious waves. At times, it was like an invisible hand was taking control of the boat.

"B" noticed and said, "Feel that? There's a little rip current out here, plus the morning breeze has things whipped up a little. This'll moderate after were clear of the Jetties."

The trainees all felt a little queasy rounding the tip of the jetties, and pretty soon all were hanging over the side being sea-sick, except Jon, who was managing to keep his down. After a while, Slim appeared from below with a plate of cut cheddar cheese. "Have some of this", Slim said setting the plate down on the *Tradewind's* teak cockpit seats."

Jon's first thought was, "Ugh, I don't know about that." But he tried it anyway. In a few minutes, it was like magic and he felt instantly better, and shortly things were smoothing out, they were clear of the Jetties and currents, and things were superb. They all felt it and could stop being worried and start enjoying this, their first time at sea and their first time sailing. Jon imagined Quintana was there, in spirit.

It was a bright sunny day, and Jon was feeling much better. The cheese worked. It was a long slow slog towards Louisiana and Vermillion bay, their first destination. But the Gulf was beautiful today. They were sailing along in not too deep water; The Gulf, as they went eastward was shallow just offshore and it became more shallow with each mile. This made the seas choppier than far out in the open ocean where the waves were longer and usually more gentle. There was plenty of active interests out there. Shrimp boats, oil service boats, drilling rigs, well platforms, helicopters overhead and a few other pleasure boats all appeared frequently.

Remembering that it was the West's first time offshore, Captain "B" decided to add extra commentary to all the goings on, and said, "This is a busy place. Will probably calm down over toward Vermillion Bay." This part of the Gulf was blue but not quite as clear as other parts of the sea due to the muddy outflow of so many rivers; the Trinity out of Galveston, the Neches and Sabine out of Port Arthur, the Calcassieu out of Lake Charles and too many to name east of there, including the Atchafalaya basin and the mighty Mississippi River basin itself.

CHAPTER 19

FINALLY AT SEA

M oca was beginning to relax a little, now out in the Gulf. She could sense the difference, being out in an unbounded sea, out of channels and other traffic. The freedom of it was exciting and a little scary to her. "What do you think sailors?" she said to the kids. They all expressed excitement.

Jon noticed Moca's attitude shift, and asked, "What's up mom? Having fun yet?"

"Yes honey, I like it!" She had a bathing suit on under shorts and was barefoot on the *Tradewinds* warm teak decks. Thinking, she said out loud, "Just think, how far this boat has been. All the way around this world. And now its carrying us." She wondered what husband Sam would think of all this.

Captain "B" ordered, "Jon, why don't you take the helm a while and give me a rest."

Jon excitedly said, "OK, I mean aye, Capt'n".

"Just hold her on this same course." Captain "B" told him, point at the compass. "Don't chase the wind too much; keep the wheel steady and don't correct too fast. You will learn to feel the shifts of wave and wind. And they are always shifting a little here and there. Just relax and steer the boat. If wind or wave starts taking over, just make a bigger shift in the heading. You can always adjust the sails if need be."

Jon's mind was working hard to grasp all this. The feel of the helm was kind of natural, especially after "B"'s advice on not chasing the helm. So this was sailing, he thought. The practical mastery of man over the elements, man over distance. He wondered what cargo, products and supplies this boat had carried to far off islands around the world in the very different waters of the South Pacific.

Captain "B" was watching Jon and noticed his thoughtful mood. "Just mind the ship and keep a sharp and constant look out all around us. Remember, be vigilant always. "He thought to tell a tale at this point. "Once I was sailing along way out in the open ocean. It was a rough patch, by golly. We had been fighting huge waves and wind feeding a big low pressure area up north of us sucking in wind for days. The seas had mounted as high as the mast. Mountainous water passing unders us. All of sudden, I glanced over the rail just to starboard to see a waterlogged telephone pole submerged floating in the water. Hit it just right, it could have easily holed the boat, or bent the rudder or propeller." His eyes had become animated and big to add effect. Jon and everybody listening were totally glued to "B's" tale and glanced to starboard just to check and imagine the site.

"Wow." Jon considered. Things got quiet after that, and they plowed on. He was having a hard time containing his imagination. He started thinking about the early spanish explorers coming in their magnificent ships just over the horizon. In these very waters but so many years ago. And later on, the privateer Jean LaFitte's ships plied these very same waters and bays. In another age, the Gulf was active in the American Civil War with both Union and Southern ships making was and conducting blockades in these waters. Finally,

World War II saw German submarines sneaking around in these waters. So the Gulf of Mexico was not just a haven for shrimp boats and oil rigs, but had seen serious business. Gulf shrimp and crab were some of the tastiest in the world, it was thought due to the outflows of muddy rivers that brought silt down from throughout america. Before they knew it they were approaching the entrance area to Vermillion Bay. This bay was the last big coastal bay in southern Louisiana before Atchafalaya and New Orleans. Since there were many oil rigs and platforms off the Louisiana coast, there were a large number of service boats plus an active fishing and shrimping industry made it a busy place.

The planned to go down outside and come back inside. That meant leave Galveston offshore thru the Gulf to Vermillion Bay, then find the Intracoastal Waterway, known as the ICW, to travel back in the ICW all the way back to Galveston. This was fine with Jon, since it would allow him to search for LaFitte's treasure on the map he had found. He just wasn't quite sure exactly which river to track.

CHAPTER 20

VERMILION BAY

"**R**eady about!" shouted Jon at the helm.
Heather, making the main sheet ready,
parroted "Ready about!"
And with that the ship made its final tack and entered
the Vermilion and Atchafalaya Bay channel. It would be a
long trip up the narrow channel. The entire Louisiana coast
west of the mouth of the Mississippi clear to the Texas border
was very shallow muddy bottom and laced with oil rigs. Far
out into the Gulf the water was still relatively shallow. Forty
miles off shore the water was still only 20 foot deep. In
contrast, forty miles off Port Aransas, Texas the Gulf was Ten
Thousand feet deep. The continental shelf was unpredictable
indeed..

They would turn on the engine and motor sail up the
channel. Unlike the Houston Ship Channel, the Vermilion
Channel had not much large shipping traffic, only shrimping
and other pleasure boats, and loud and irritating oil service
boats that constantly buzzed in and out to the offshore
coastal rigs from Morgan City.

Jon had been reading a book about Vermilion bay that offered the following:

The Vermilion River is a bayou in South Louisiana that flows through the towns of Perry, Abbeville and Lafayette and the little community of Long Bridge. It empties into Vermilion Bay after crossing the Intracoastal Waterway near Intracoastal City.

About 2 miles upstream from Vermilion Bay the Vermilion River crosses the Intracoastal Waterway. Eight miles upstream from Vermilion Bay the Vermilion River passes the Port of Vermilion and 15 miles upstream of Vermilion Bay it passes through Perry Louisiana. Seventeen miles upstream of Vermilion Bay the Vermilion River passes through the town of Abbeville.

About 3 miles upstream from Lafayette, The Ruth Canal empties into the Vermilion River after beginning from Bayou Teche near Ruth. Approximately 5 miles upstream from Lafayette the Vermilion River passes through the little community of Long Bridge. During the 1970's the several permanently closed bridges that crossed the Vermilion River at various places (The Breaux Bridge Highway, Carmel Drive in Long Bridge, East Gloria Switch Road and Old Highway 726) were choked with trash making it impossible to continue upstream any farther.

As of April, 2004 it is possible to go upstream for about 19 miles before a bridge is reached which is obstructed with trash (mostly tree branches).

So up they headed.

CHAPTER 21

HOMEWARD THROUGH THE INTRACOASTAL

Captain "B" had decided to return "inside" through the Intracoastal Waterway to make good time rather than "outside" offshore in the Gulf, plus to show the trainee's a new path. That was fine with Jon, because it represented new waters to know about and it agreed with his plans to explore lands indicated on his map. Captain "B" had met a local man named Destrehan Foret who seemed to have a lot of local knowledge and he was aboard *Tradewind* at the Captain's request to help advise. Down below, "B", Jon, Moca and Destrehan were gathered around the chart table discussing the route and looking at marine waterway maps, which they had learned were called "charts".

Jon remarked, "Capt'n "B", the charts show so many creeks and sloughs and wide spots that cross and join the ICW along in here. How are we going to ever find our way, even WITH these charts?"

"Yup, between Port Arthur and New Orleans, navigating the ditch (Intracoastal) can get very very confusing, as I remember, and as I see it here." instructed "B". Especially around and east of Morgan City, Louisiana you get into where the ditch is going through woods and swamps with many false channels and sloughs, and your view is blocked, like a winding water-path through the forest; a real maze! Best to follow a push boat on your first trip through there! Keep that in mind. But don't be tempted to lash-up to them or be towed by them; you're bound to damage the boat if you do." Jon filed that away.

"*Yeah, da ditch go tru dat Atchafalya River basin swamp, de larges swamp in de United State. Easy get loss in dere!*" Destrehan cautioned with raised eyebrows and a cajun-serious set to his cajun face.

"B" went on, "Well, all that's all east of here and for another trip, Jon. For now, from here in Vermilion Bay, we'll proceed west down the ICW and not too far, forty mile or so, we will be crossing the Calcasieu River." The Calcasieu was in the vicinity of the modern southwestern Louisiana town of Lake Charles, Louisiana where he wanted to explore Contraband bayou, a smallish bayou the ran off the river, right into the city. The old maps were rough approximations, due to lack of technology back in the days of Lafitte, so he would have to take that into consideration. After that, it was a long straight shot as the ditch cut through salt marshes to the Sabine River, which divided Louisiana and Texas.

Destrehan Foret chimed in his heavy Cajun drawl, "*Yeah sha, dat saal marsh, she full of da bess fishin', crab, an duck you can imagine, yeah. Also, dere's lot'o oil activity down dere too, .. lots! You got to watch for dem tug boat and dem barge, dey run all da time, yeah.*"

At the bottom of Sabine River it joined the Neches River just at the upper region of Sabine Lake. They planned to take the Neches River up to Beaumont, where they would dock up at Beaumont's riverfront park near downtown Beaumont.

Jon could then take a small boat further up the river to find and explore Ten-Mile Slough.

After staying in Beaumont several days, they would return back down the river, rejoin the ICW down through Port Arthur and on back to Galveston and up to homeport in Clear Lake. So that was the plan.

Dealing with Intracoastal Waterway is a regular feature of sailing along the east coast of the US, and especially along the gulf coast, at least down through about Pensacola, Florida. It was fast and safe, assuming one could avoid confrontation with one of the hundreds of tug boats pushing barges. It is federally controlled and mandated to an approximate depth of 9 feet and 100 feet wide with usually a muddy bottom and shoaled in sometimes in certain places. In certain points, it touches the open gulf, has tidal locks, shares space and overlays major shipping channels, and traverses major rivers, including the mighty Mississippi. These points can be especially "gamey" for the casual mariner. It is commonly referred to as "the ditch".

The "ditch" was a marvel of modern marine transportation, even though it was quite old now; it continued to be well maintained by a variety of Federal governmental agencies. It was the life blood stream of essential petrochemical products travelling from one marine terminal to another, from one giant petrochemical plant or refinery to another.

CHAPTER 22

SAFE HARBOR - OR NOT

Jon was at the helm, of course with Captain Bellwether standing by. But nothing much was going on except a tired crew. Moca was below straightening and cleaning the galley and salon. *Tradewind* motored in through the Kemah channel and on through the lake to Safe Shore. They rounded the channel turning into the marina and passed the lighthouse, which marked Harbor's entrance. The view of the marina harbor of Safe Shore was blocked from the lake by condominiums and trees. Now in the marina proper, Jon could see something going on. TV media trucks, and throngs of people. It seemed to be focused on their area of the marina.

Turning down their row of boat slips the crush of greeters ran to the end of their peer to follow them home. *Tradewind* was on all slow while Jon and Captain "B" deftly backed her into her slip. The crew jumped off and some of the kids threw off dock lines to them. *Tradewind* was home and tied up.

Marina security people had block off the immediate area around the boat but the pressing crowd was all packed on the main pier vying position and attention. In the crowd, Jon could see a lot of non-press people he recognized who were just there to say welcome home. But the gold-treasure adventure part of the story was fuelling the flames of everybody. And the news was big indeed: Jean Lafitte's treasure, or at least part of it, had been found; and it mainly belonged to the finder, Mr. Jon West and crew! And everybody wanted to see it and have some kind of contact with Jon or the family or the crew.

People are innately drawn to celebrity. Like powerful magnets.

In this case, it was a little hard to tell who or what was the main attraction: the gold or the people or the story ... or all of it! Who could tell? None of the principals were in any way ready for this type of attention. They all kind of hovered around the boat, not wanting to be first to actually make contact with the information and contact hungry throngs. They didn't quite know what to say, what not to say or how to say it. Cameras and microphones are scary to most folks, but they knew they were going be facing them head on sooner or later, and it seemed to be sooner.

Moca looked over at Bob in the next slip, who had his head poked out of *Dama's* companionway, like a prairie dog half-in and half-out of his hole, looking around at the melee. He caught Moca's eye, shook and bowed his head and was smiling-laughing in disbelief and irony. Moca just smiled back and gave a small knowing wave hello.

Captain "B" was the first to venture across the security line right where the CNN and KGAL-TV crew were set-up.

"We can't say exactly where we found the loot. Everybody would be in there hunting. It would ruin the place; and besides, it's very dangerous to go around those rivers and bays and bayous and sloughs in small boats. There's gators, and traps and trotlines and crab-traps to mention a few." Jon said to the reporter. "People would get lost, and flat out disappear and never be heard from again. The gold we found is supposed to worth about five million dollars, by today's price. And it sat there for all those years safe and sound, until Jean Lafitte's map showed me where to go, and it was not an easy place; we were lucky!"

The place turned out to be called Ten-Mile Slough up the Neches River north of the I-10 bridge, off the main river to the right about 3 miles up. The first one or two miles up the slough was a swamp load with Cypress knees and trees and water. No banks at all. Then, a bank seemed to rise out of the water, on both sides. All this was evident on the map that Jon had. And it showed the slight hill on the left bank with the treasure on the other side of hill in a grove of trees, buried. It was well concealed and no one would think to be digging back there. Precious few people even went that far back on ten-mile slough, to fish or camp, or trap.

CHAPTER 23

Trip to Port Isabel and Arrival

The *Tradewind* plowed on. It took most of the day just to clear Freeport which was southward down the coast from Galveston. Most of the accompanying boats were dropping away like flies due to the very very rough conditions. Jon showered on deck from the solar shower to get refreshed and ready for the night. Thank God for the experienced crew. The next days and nights at sea were astounding to the West family trainees. He was on first watch along with crewman Fred, but would probably be too excited to sleep. As *Tradewind* and two other vessels sailed on into the night, the winds stiffened a little and the seas built. Eleven vessels from the sailing club had begun the trip, but seven of them had ducked in at the Freeport jetties due to the rotten offshore conditions. It turned out there was a massive low pressure area stalled and deepening over the upper central US. It had been there building for about a week, and it was drawing a persistent and strong south wind all the way from down towards the Yucatan Peninsula and straight across the Gulf. It was causing unstable weather, strong winds and localized thunderstorms, and causing mountainous seas to build over the normal patterns. All this was right over the route to Port Isabel.

This night, the next day and night were filled with constant pounding waves, lashing spray, occasional thunderstorms and generally being thrown about the boat and hanging on. Very little was eaten or drank, except by the experienced crew who knew the ropes. Slim had made up a supply of sandwiches in the galley. There were strong-eyes and a safety belt made fast in the galley to allow cooking in a seaway, but the rest of the West family trainees tended to find a seat or a bunk and just wedge-in to keep from being thrown about as the ship galloped and plunged and pounded from monstrous wave after monstrous wave.

Moca, wedged down in a cockpit seat said loudly over the weather, "Now I see what this dodger is for. Before, I thought it kind of blocked the view, but now, gotta have one!" As the waves crashed on the bow, massive spray would slam the protective plasticine windshield called a dodger, to "dodge" the spray.

Momentarily, Captain "B" poked his head out of the companionway and said, "Fred, you and Jon go forward and reef-in the Genoa sail some more. She's goin' too fast." Captain "B" could tell everything even from down below in his bunk. The front sail provided most of the wind drive for the vessel, with the other sails providing mostly stability and balance, depending on the point of sail of course. By way of imparting some knowledge to the trainees, "B" looked at Jon and said, "That sail is a compromise and is meant for much lower winds. She's got a pouch in her that's scooping too much wind. Roll her up some more, maybe two or three rolls. Get her well past that damn pocket!"

All were harnessed on to the ship, a rule for night running.

Jack-lines were always rigged from bow to stern allowing crew to travel the entire length of the ship both port and starboard and stay lashed on to avoid going overboard. Any crew going overboard, even in more moderate conditions at night, would surely be lost.

"Rule number one," Said Fred, "keep the water out and the crew aboard!

Hook on and let's go up, Jon." Fred went ahead, with Jon following more carefully. It was a trick to even navigate the deck, which was constantly awash with sea. Up forward, the bow pitched violently and at times would plunge into a wave and be knee deep in seawater. Both men had to hold themselves down on the deck to keep from going airborne and getting thrown off or hurt. The maneuver required coordination from the helmsman where Captain "B" had temporarily taken over while Fred was forward. He would have to head-up into the wind briefly to take pressure off the sail so it could be rolled in.

Jon felt and heard the pressure ease and took in the reef past the damn pocket and made fast the control lines. Then he watched a minute, taking in the astonishing surroundings of the awesome weather and the vast and angry seas. Finally he inched back to the safety and relative sanity of the cockpit.

Captain "B" gave the helm back to Fred, while Jon hunkered down on the other cockpit seat. He said to Moca, "It's awesome up there! Exciting, but not a place to hang around in these conditions." In calm conditions, he liked to go up there, lay on the bow and gaze up at the massive Genoa sail and feel the wind drive the boat. But right now, it was pitching cold and wet hell up there. Adjustment done, Capt'n "B" was satisfied and went back down below for more rest, and normal storm chaos returned, with the ship slightly calmer in the blow now.

Finally about 4 a.m. on the second night, winds began

to moderate and the sea was turning into sloppy leftovers. Captain "B" started the *Tradewind's* powerful diesel engine to provide drive through the sloppy choppy directionless waves, but left up the sails to provide a little stability. Jon made note that there was a counter strategy to each of the many varied conditions a ship could meet, and that Capt'n "B" had to call on those strategies and enable them timely, to stay ahead of conditions as best possible.

As dawn broke, Port Isabel was nicely ahead on the horizon, a flat low lying coast with the channel markers, the black and white lighthouse, the big Queen Isabella Causeway bridge over to South Padre Island, and a few high rise hotels being the welcoming marks of civilization. The moderating seas were still lumpy left-overs from the weather, and it was still totally cloudy.

Capt'n "B" 's navigation had been flawless and as the *Tradewind* passed the jetties entrance marker buoy, Jon silently reflected that they were now in, or at least near the outflowing waters of the Rio Grande. It is the historic river that marked the boundaries between Texas and Mexico, that ran almost up to Colorado. A river of dreams and movies was the Rio Grande. Once past the jetties they turned right at the entrance to the southernmost end of the Intracoastal Waterway and the entrance to that water-desert known as the Laguna Madre which lay between the outer barrier island, Padre Island, and the Texas mainland. Their destination marina was not far now. The gloomy clouds were beginning to burn off. A more tropical sunny day was revealed along with nice sandy blueish green water, definitely different than the muddy bayous and waters around Galveston.

"Are we there yet?", said one of the tired kids.

"Yes!" Jon replied, has he was telling Capt'n "B" some of the history, as he had remembered from his reading and research. Jon always did his research.

Captain "B" ordered, "Jon, go check the decks and lines - make ready for landing. Make everything ready, we'll be landing to take on fuel before birthing.

Spirits were lifting and all were now on deck eager with anticipation, although it would still be about a half-hour before they arrived at the fuel dock. Jon was learning that the captain should always be several steps ahead in the agenda, to live in multiple worlds simultaneously and seamlessly, that of the immediate "now" and also the time and need ahead. They would need the fuel and supplies for their return trip back up the coast "just in case".

Jon continued on with his history, "The lighthouse was built in 1852 and even had a role in the Civil War and was at times on either side. The town was named by General Zachary Taylor. A lot of people came through here during the California gold rush days. Several hurricanes made landfall here and the place has been destroyed and rebuilt before. In 1519, Spanish explorers documented being here." It was impossible to sail the Texas coast without visualizing Spanish Galleons on the horizon, the first white men to ever visit and settle into this region of the planet. "There are sunken Spanish ships still being found in the Texas coastal waters to this day."

As the *Tradewind* took on fuel at the fuel dock, Jon reflected, "Wow, that was some trip! I can now see why everything on a ship needs to be very much stronger than you would think it would ever need to be. The strength of materials, the way things are done, the way things are fastened together, the way things are stored away and secured, the way hulls are crafted, just everything!".

Captain "B" chuckled, "Yes sir, yes sir, everything is right! Gotta watch out for the weak-link principle." He was somehow proud of Jon's insight. "And you stood up well back out there, might I say. Showed no fear, but I think you gain some respect for what madam sea can throw up at you."

Jon re-pictured mountain after mountain of huge sea that had marched under the valiant ship as she sailed on the lively winds into the dark night, so true on her course to this spot. Crafted by man, and so persistent in purpose to carry crew, passengers and cargo safely in all conditions. The ships design and equipment crafted from historic experience man's ability to persevere and use tools to exist and explore his realm. "I wonder why some ships sink in storms, Capt'n?" Jon queried.

"Mostly they run aground or something breaks.", Captain "B" mused offhandedly. "Unless you wind up in extreme conditions, surf down a wave and pitch-pole or roll three-sixty and founder the vessel". He went on, confessing, "during long tricks at the helm on dark nights as a young skipper, I used to go down long lists in my head of what could go wrong, what could break, picturing parting shrouds that held up the masts, picturing each and every thru-hull fitting that was about to fail or pop out letting in the sea, or even the hull splitting in two!" he said laughing. "Damn! Near wore myself out! Oh well, I guess it was some sort of perverse entertainment on those lonely nights. I would be mentally rehearsing what I would do if each of these things happened. Finally got tired of such mental charades. Sort of decided, I could handle them as they came, or whatever was going to happen would just happen. Then the crew or I just would handle it. We all have our demons, but we can't live in fear, but just be the best prepared we can. What the hell else can a man do?".

Jon thought, *yes what the hell else?* Fears and demons he pondered. "Being prepared, being ahead of it, that's the best one can do.", he offered.

"Right, you're right on boy." gruffed Captain "B", "Stow

the irrational, put the fears and demons overboard but trust instinct and seaman's intuition, and damn well be prepared. And don't forget about the big "why" question."

"What do you mean, Capt'n "B"?".

"B" continued, "Why are you out there in the first place? Not where you're going or how you're going, but *WHY* are you going. Did Edison want to invent light bulbs, or light the dark? Did Columbus want to have a nice sail or find China? I guess what I'm sayin' is to be sure your goal is worthy, to be sure you always know the *WHY* of a thing."

As Jon mulled this weighty thought, the fueling finished and they made way for the marina, where they would be for few days. He thought about the real danger of even a short journey like they had just finished from Galveston to Port Isabel, hundreds of miles offshore, in water miles deep. Exposure to all kinds of risks. Why, he wondered, really, why? Captain "B" 's one-word question was actually as deep as that water they'd crossed. Something else to file away for later consideration.

Their spot was not far and soon they were pulling in. They set up to counteract the sea breeze blowing and the walk of the prop in reverse, which moved the stern to port, but there was also an invisible current of a changing tide that caused the vessel to move to port too much and the clanged the dock a little too hard, bending something sticking out from the ship.

Jon, still musing, said, "What if he just liked inventing, or Columbus actually just liked sailing? What if they really did just want fame? What if they like all those aspects? What if there was some other hidden agenda that nobody knows about?" The question would have to hang unanswered.

Just then, Captain "B" let out an expletive, "damn, I didn't see that current on these floating docks. An easy fix though, Jon, re-bend that after we're tied. Always watch the tide current, it'll overpower the breeze usually." He hated silly mistakes, although it could be extremely hard to read a current. Let it be known that ye see'd Capt'n B make a small oversight! Not ashamed to admit it. Although most marinas are sheltered and block currents, this one's a flow-through, kind of sticking out."

"Now ready for a little land-tourist adventure!" Said Moca, as the West's crowded into a taxi and rode up to the Brownsville, Texas - Matamoros, Mexico crossing border crossing point for their foray into their first foreign country. Going through customs was no big deal, and a lot, in fact most looked like they did this pass daily as part of their routine lives, rather that tourists. "You kids watch out for each other while we're over here. There have been some weird reports and some kidnappings over here in the news over the last few years, so plan on me hanging onto you all! I'm just telling you now."

"OK, Mom." several replied at once, "Fine, but can we buy some Mexican stuff?" said one them.

"I want one of those whips!" Heather chimed in.

Kit said, "No, those are for boys! Get me one."

"And remember, do NOT drink any water there! None! No ice either!" cautioned Moca.

After crossing the border, they strolled in tight formation into the shopping area, obviously set there for the tourists, with a lot of street vendors, garish signs, little Mexican kids approaching them yelling "Chiclets, Chiclets, candy?" or otherwise begging money. Moca waved them away with a stern mother-lion look, like swatting flies. They were in a strange land and like most border towns, a dirty land. Her instincts told her they should not linger or stay too long there.

But they proceeded to walk through shop after shop of the cheap *tourista* type Mexican goods. Onyx and wooden chess sets, bongo drums, mariachis, conga drums, sombrero hats, Indian type blankets, leather goods of all sorts, and tropical looking clothing. On the corner outside a nicer store played a mariachi band and Moca placed a dollar into the kitty and smiled at them. Kit spied a whip and handed it to Moca. Heather settled for some non-tunable bongo drums that had real skins and stave's of tropical wood. She purchased these items along with a couple of shirts for herself and one to send back to Lana at college. Moca saw a liquor store and stopped in to buy Captain "B" and crew a couple of bottles of their favorite libation. They had shopped too long, and it was getting dark. Leaving the last shop, they were walking back to the border crossing when she noticed a fancy van parked on their side of the narrow street, with some dangerous looking "hombres" standing around. They would have to walk right through them, as she glanced around for alternate routes. There were none. She held onto the little ones tightly and plowed ahead. One of the hombres started to come towards them, when two men in black suits stepped out of nowhere and stood like towers blocking the bad men, who quickly retreated, got into the van and drove away.

Suddenly from behind, a familiar voice boomed, "Ma'am, y'all best get on back to the other side now ya 'hey ah'" as he as quickly disappeared into another big black official looking SUV that quickly headed to the same crossing.

It was none other than the Brunson truck man!

CHAPTER 24

HOME AGAIN!

The voyage home was long but uneventful, except for a heck of a storm crossing Matagorda Bay. They were almost across the Bay when the storm overtook them. The waves in that bay became so intense that Jon thought he would see the bottom between the steep waves any minute. A tug boat travelling close to them carrying an empty barge came on the radio reporting that he had lost the barge, so everybody watch out. The *Tradewind* had to circle an ICW Channel marker until the visibility clear enough for them to make it all the way back across the bay, and spend the night moored up in Port O'Connor. To say the storm was intense was an understatement.

Once back home, the boat was parked and washed down good, everything wrapped, anchored, tied up ready for riding out weather fronts, or whatever including the starting the next trip. It was as if the boat had a spirit that want everything to be put in a very certain way, to make the spirit rest comfortably, to gain energy, for the next trip. Making the spirit rested and strong would somehow keep the passengers and crew safe on the next trip.

Actually, the spirit of the boat had good reason to be tired, and want everything put to sleep right and neatly and orderly. The boat had new crew, new masters, and had been navigating new waters along the Gulf Coast. Even helping to discover part of a treasure buried centuries ago. What else would the future hold Jon West mulled, and the *Tradewind*? *When, if ever, will I get to see Quintana again? Will my dad, Sam, ever return?* And who was that Brunson truck guy, anyway?

The End

Printed in the United States
By Bookmasters